SAVE THE SILVER BULLET

To Redders,

with thanks,

SAVE THE
SILVER
BULLET

The small steps to successful transformation

BEN DE HALDEVANG

I have been incredibly lucky to have worked with some extraordinary people over the years.

This book is dedicated to those who continue to inspire me – from the round table above Sweetings to the glass box in Amoy Street and more recently the Zoom gallery.

Publisher's note

ISBN: 978-1-5272-9937-5

Contents

INTRODUCTION

February 25, 2018, found me striding down the sparkling third fairway on Gullane No1, probably my favorite hole in the world. My drive was long, and, although my fellow golfers were making all the right noises, I knew that I had fallen prey to the old man's mistake of not quite finishing my swing. I was still confident that I would find my ball nestled to the right of the bunker, but the closer I got the more I was gripped by the fear that plagues most amateur golfers. I forced myself to imagine what Tiger would do in the same situation...except he never would be in this situation! I was struck by the thought that, when it comes to golf, Tiger and I sit at opposite ends of the strategy and implementation challenge.

For the sake of clarity, let's define these terms. Strategy is, according to the *Oxford English Dictionary*, a plan of action designed to achieve a long-term or overall aim; and implementation is the process of putting a decision or plan into effect.

The thing about Tiger is that he doesn't think about implementation at all. His stroke is almost always perfect, so his focus is on strategy. He asks the following questions: 'What do I want the ball to do?' and 'What do I need to account for (wind, weather, underfoot conditions, and lie)?'

By contrast, a beginner at golf finds even the most fundamental of strategic decisions, such as which club to use, entirely irrelevant as to distance, direction, and shape of flight. For the new golfer, it's all about implementation: what are the hips doing, what about the grip?

How does that analogy play out in the world of transformation? The cynic might say that the leadership of companies would like to believe that their organizations are a lot like Tiger. In fact, they are probably a lot more like the beginner. When you speak to senior and mid-level managers within those organizations who have responsibility for transformation programs, there is no naivety about their assessment of the track record and capability. They will point to key weaknesses existing within their business that have led to poor results. The answers are reasonably consistent, and more often than not relate to the intangible, not the rational or strategic. Consistent examples are poor retention of important employees, slow decision making at leadership level, and inefficient processes that are no longer fit for purpose. A quote from a managing director of a global investment bank with more than twenty years' experience provides a good summary of the issue:

> 'In my tenure, I cannot think of a single strategic proposal which we've acted upon as an organization that has ever been implemented in the way it was initially intended....not successfully, anyway.'

So, if it's not naivety and it's not a lack of knowledge or ignorance, what is the cause of this false optimism about internal capability? More importantly, how do we counter it?

Returning to my golf analogy, what should I do? I have three options:

- Fix it by having some lessons. *In corporate terms, take some advice and listen to the internal messages.*
- Aim down the left side of the fairway in the hope that my slice will carry the ball onto the short stuff. *Compensate for internal weakness by providing more support and time.*
- Aim down the middle, on the basis that one out of ten shots will go straight! *Ignore all the above and continue to make the same mistakes.*

Like many amateur golfers, and most companies, I tend to the final option and hope for the best. While the impact of false optimism on a golf course is hardly fatal, its impact in the corporate world is likely to be altogether more disastrous.

What role does the program manager play in this destructive circle of denial and repetition? The artefacts that we are taught to produce lend credibility to our processes. The reality, however, is that they present a degree of linear certainty around execution that is both unhelpful and unrealistic. Just focusing for a moment on the world of transformation arising from mergers and acquisitions, they are:

- Unhelpful, because, even with the most detailed due diligence process our actual knowledge of the target and ultimate business requirements is going to be flawed. Building an implementation plan based on partial information is not going to make delivery any easier.

▶ Unrealistic, because they are based on assumptions that have never actually been validated with those internal subject matter experts who are tasked with the responsibility of implementation.

My insight on that glorious day in February was intuitive at best, and needed to be tested. Over the next twelve months I interviewed more than 120 program directors to hear their stories of success and failure, looking for themes of 'what' influenced performance.

These stories show that, contrary to market understanding, the irrational, emotional nature of decision making in humans is identical to that which takes place in companies. It seems that we need to bring the 'human' back into implementation.

What might you hope to gain from spending some of your precious time reading stories about people you've never heard of, in places you may never visit, and in circumstances you probably won't face? Let me set out my three intentions:

▶ Ideas, insights, and practical solutions to some universal issues from the world of program and project management.

▶ Entertainment and *Schadenfreude in equal measure. As human beings we are positively disposed to a good story, whether it ends on a positive note or in disaster. These stories are about characters who are faced with extraordinary, unplanned, and unimagined situations. You will also read about some remarkable solutions to these problems.*

▶ *'We got there by coincidence, not by design.'* You will get an insight into the unplanned, the unstructured, the irrational and emotional experience faced by those with implementation responsibilities. In short, an 'under the bonnet' perspective of the chaotic roller coaster that is usually masked by those artefacts of implementation, the plan, the GANTT chart, the Risk and Issues Register!

A few health warnings:

▶ If you're expecting a magical framework that is going to solve all your implementation problems, you're going to be disappointed. At the core of this book is a set of stories from various perspectives with all the challenges of post-rationalization, poor memory, and false optimism. With some reluctance, I have set out some guidelines that are consistent with some different approaches to transformation, but there is no 'silver bullet' in this book.

If you are expecting to read stories from 'famous' people, read no further. The interviewees come from a very wide universe, geographically, sectorially, and demographically. With the exception of Mike DeNoma, it is extremely unlikely that you will have heard of any of them. They are exceptional, authentic, dedicated, and extremely intelligent people who believe in what they do and have great experience. Best of all, they are prepared to share their stories with us, but they live in the world of implementation, which does not do 'famous'.

Throughout the rest of the book there are numerous stories and insights from my conversations. I add context early and where it is required. Clearly much of the editing is down to what I heard from my interviews and thought was particularly insightful. Over the course of my research, I've interviewed more than 120 people and have more than 140 hours of recording.

If you are looking for more golf analogies, put this book down and head to the range. I don't apologize for my sporting start to the book. It's where I began to think about the challenge of implementation and delivery. However, it would be artifice to stretch such an analogy further.

01
THE MODEL AND
THE CONTEXT

In 1999 I started a consulting business aimed at supporting companies going through mergers and acquisitions in the critical post-deal integration period. The thought that execution and program delivery might somehow diverge from the strategic intent was implicitly understood by many leaders at the time but rarely admitted. There was anecdotal evidence as to what caused deals to fail and a recognition that buying businesses was risky, but no one considered an approach that looked at implementation capability first, before deciding on strategy.

Part of our consulting business success came from a perspective on program management that recognized the inherent challenges of the deal process. This was a process where the exercise of gaining knowledge about the target and making decisions about the future state were entirely independent of each other. Not only were the individuals and teams from different parts of the business, but they did not seem to spend much time communicating with each other on findings. It was a process where the future plan was based on assumptions, made up to a year before, which were never revised as the data and forecasting capacity advanced.

Our simple insight was that by becoming more responsive to actual information, the results would improve. Hardly rocket science!

One of the comments regarding that period in the early 2000s made by a senior corporate strategy director with over twenty years' global M&A experience was particularly appropriate: '99% of acquisitions are essentially retail therapy for CEOs.' Having a deal on one's curriculum vitae in those days was a key credential for any aspiring CEO.

Some might argue that not much has changed in the world of mergers and acquisitions.

I disagree.

There have been real changes across the landscape of transformation that have undoubtedly improved success rates.

▸ The advent of a holistic perspective to human capital and cultural change. This is perhaps the most surprising shift. Today, people and culture feature highly in most transformation programs as key success factors.
▸ The adoption of 'agile'-based methodology to program and project management. This is an acknowledgement that the way to complete complex programs of work is through a series of small, highly responsive, iterative and flexible steps.
▸ A step away from the 'one stop shop' approach to M&A integration with an acknowledgement that there are different ways to deliver value in a deal. An acceptance that there are other forms of collaboration that might be as effective as a deal.
▸ The commitment to innovation with companies dedicating resources, time, and leadership to finding new solutions to existing problems and future opportunities.
▸ A recognition that today's employees are motivated by different factors, work in different ways, and have different expectations of their employer. This is reflected in the revival of social entrepreneurial businesses. These organizations recognize the need for balance between the needs of the community they serve, their shareholders, and their employees, and proactively strive to manage this. The impact of Covid-19 has further accentuated this need for balance.
▸ The adoption of behavioral economics as a relevant discipline for transformation. This is a discipline that can provide a valuable insight into human strengths and weaknesses, how we make decisions, and how we respond to change.

That's the good news!

The bad news is that the challenges are not getting any smaller:

▸ Organizations continue to expand their transformation portfolio of work. In terms of digital transformation activities, IDC (International Data Corporation, a subsidiary of IDG) predicts global investment of $6.8 trillion over the next three years with 65% of the world's GDP to be digitized. In 2020, despite the undoubted impact of Covid-19 on M&A, global volumes exceeded $3.6 trillion, a 5% dip on 2019.

► Performance continues to be terrible. By any measure (delivery of business benefits as defined in the scope of work, customer engagement levels) not much has changed in the last ten years. Between 70% and 90% of post-deal integration or transformation programs do not deliver the desired benefits (*Harvard Business Review* 2019). On the subject of measurement, the actual returns achieved are subject to considerable debate and downright manipulation. There is still a lack of transparency that is quite surprising. Ask any Finance Director / CFO about their method of calculating revenue synergies in a deal, and you'll understand how opaque the process of attributing benefits remains.

► Those who are needed to deliver transformation, the employees, don't want to. The global employee base is at a historically low level of engagement. In 2020, a challenging year given the circumstances, the data from Gallop suggests that 85% of employees are 'not actively engaged or actively disengaged at work.'

► The short-term mindset of leadership due to tenure and financial incentives is increasingly at odds with the longer-term strategic requirements of companies. Put in simple terms, according to PwCs strategy management consulting business, Strategy&, average CEO tenure is five years. The average publicized period of return for M&A is three and a half years. but anecdotal evidence would suggest that the impact on performance is in excess of five years.

At the heart of this book there are two key questions that need to be addressed to change this picture.

1. Is it possible to identify the conditions for success?
2. Are these replicable, and if so how?

Given that we often learn much more from failure than success, I am also going to address the other side of these questions: What are the conditions that consistently deliver failure?

Another framework?

I am not a big fan of frameworks. From my experience, they are created retrospectively in glorious hindsight. They are built on the basis of false optimism and no small degree of myopia. Their applicability to any future situation is questionable. There is also a very human tendency, often driven out of despair, which confuses frameworks with 'silver bullets.' When a program subsequently fails to deliver the required result, it is the framework that takes the hit. The caveats that any framework designer puts in place are conveniently ignored.

An example:

The corporate world is littered with knowledge management delivery programs that have fundamentally failed, based on take-up rates post implementation. Given the intent of the leadership and best efforts of the implementation team, why does this happen? For the simple reason that 'my' challenge is always going to be more complex, more intractable, with more difficult stakeholders, than 'yours'!

What value is there, then, in developing another framework? I have three reasons, one practical and two helpful.

- ▸ From a practical perspective, while I would love to share chapter and verse in terms of the stories I've heard, we need some kind of structure, and I have therefore created something that hangs together around key themes and ideas.
- ▸ This framework stems not from a design but from a delivery perspective. These are fundamentally different starting points. The former seeks to use rational, logical thinking to break down complexity and create a clear, linear flow of decision points and influencing factors. The latter uses the learning from the actual experience of implementation to understand the messy, haphazard world of iteration, informal, non-hierarchical communication, and tactical thinking that dominate the process.
- ▸ With this focus on delivery, there is an opportunity to understand the context, the conditions surrounding implementation and the structure *within your own organization*.

Taking the lessons from this book and applying them in the context of your own organization is not a passive process. It requires a bit of introspection and some collaboration. I would encourage you to break down the challenge into three steps:

- *Spend some time thinking deeply about your organization.*
- *Understand the challenges and opportunities of transformation within your organization.*
- *Share these openly with those you trust and respect.*

Program managers...who they are, where they come from, what they do

No one, in my experience, decides to become a program manager when they leave school! In the vast majority of cases it is still a role that is part, or perhaps the end point, of a random, unplanned journey through a career. For most program managers the qualification for the next role is the experience and perceived success or failure of the last program. The criteria by which they are selected are not always relevant and often misleading.

- Externally perceived complexity is often based on size and scale. While these are relevant to some degree, complexity arises in a myriad other ways, as we shall discover in this book.
- A focus on the sector in which the program manager has worked. It is true that sector knowledge helps with specific language. Speaking this language helps in interview. It may also help in the very early stages of understanding scope. Sector expertise on its own, however, is not going to guarantee success. Curiosity, appreciative inquiry, and a willingness to ask questions (and if necessary the same question many times and in many ways) are the real skill sets you need.

It is fair to say that while program management wasn't on the school careers advice list, there is more familiarity in my generation than in previous ones with the concept of transformation. Our exposure to mergers and acquisitions has been a formative part of our career. Much of our corporate experience has been marked by major corporate upheaval, a process for which we were largely unprepared.

Paul Siegenthaler was a key architect in the creation of Diageo from the merger of Guinness and Grand Met in 1997, the most transformative deal in the drinks industry and one that led the way for many others to follow. He describes that experience well:

> '*I started in a family business and expected to be working there until I retired or died! But nine years into that job, perhaps my saving grace because it was becoming a bit boring, United Distillers decided they would consolidate their distributors by buying one and binning the rest. The resulting company was four times larger as a consequence.*
>
> *That was my first experience of integration, my first experience of moving from family allegiance into corporate governance. That happened in the late 1980s, and two years later I was the only MD left who had been 'bought.' All the others had failed to adapt, change their mindset, were unable to see what was going to happen. And that sort of qualified me to transform other businesses which they'd bought but which weren't going well.*'

He talks about the selection process for future M&A integration programs:

> '*Why did they choose me? I'd gone through the journey myself, so I knew what it entailed. The other reason was simply that I had some language skills, and the others didn't. By the time Guinness and GrandMet merged to form Diageo in 1997, I was the only country general manager and part of the European executive team that had restructured companies in three different countries. Both of my bosses felt that they wanted a non-Brit to manage the whole of Europe, so that European country based teams couldn't hide behind their nationality as a way of delaying or avoiding change. So it was a mix of personal and corporate experience and cross-cultural sensitivity.*'

This random career concept in transformation / M&A is a theme rather than a coincidence.

David Cox was the COO at a highly innovative, customer-centric Spanish Telco before he started on the journey of becoming a subject matter expert in customer experience transformation programs. He does still work in Telco but has worked on most continents across emerging and mature markets.

David Boyd trained as an engineer and joined British Steel as a graduate. He got his first project management opportunity because they were looking for French-speakers. He has regularly moved from corporate life (digital director, international with Clear Channel, one of the world's largest outdoor advertising businesses) to consultancy and back again, with his current role as CEO of a pharmaceuticals consulting business. He encapsulates the fluidity of career path which is common to most program managers.

Chris Sykes, Dean Cleland, and a couple of others began their adult lives in the military before moving into the Financial Services sector where they've operated in senior Program Director / leadership roles in financial services for the last twenty years.

Kish Gill, Herbin Chia, Abhay Pande, and Alastair Campbell came from strategy consulting, in Kish's case in-house, while the others started their careers in consulting. All three found a need, an interest, and an opportunity to move from strategy / corporate development and into the world of implementation.

For David Malligan, Geoff Fyte, Conrad Trinidad, and many others, the route to program leadership started in the world of technology. This is not surprising. The roll-out of technology is perhaps the original birthplace for the program management discipline and with the advent of 'agile,' remains a place of innovation.

For Gordon Craig, James Berry, and Nick Keppel-Palmer, the challenges of starting up businesses and growing them to sizeable, market leading, and highly innovative organizations led them to core program management disciplines. The single purpose vehicle or start-up has many similarities to a transformation program.

For Ian Joshua and Sandip Joshi, the initial start in banking led to ever more challenging banking-led programs of work. The shift to an increasingly compliance-led approach to the financial sectors has given them a broad range of transformation experience, albeit within a narrow sector focus.

Probably the largest group started their lives in the world of consulting, often within the big four audit firms of Pricewaterhousecoopers, Deloitte, EY, and KPMG. Even in that consulting environment, where planning is the 'bread and butter' of paid work, the program management discipline has not been highly regarded until relatively recently. Many of those with whom I spoke have had to compromise in terms of the pace of career progression as a result of their choice of subject matter expertise.

For this group, despite all their experience of planning and implementation, the shock of 'owning' delivery is still significant. Karl Godderis, who started his career with PwC in Belgium and then spent ten years consulting in Indonesia before embarking on a fascinating set of post-acquisition integration program roles in that country, perhaps puts it best:

> *'When you come out of a consulting environment, you think that life is one big methodology. When you then start working with people going through change, it becomes clear very quickly that it's not...it is a truly enlightening experience.'*

A fluid but fulfilling career

Once in the world of program management, however, people stay. With very few exceptions, those I interviewed had more than ten years' experience in program management, and over 50% had more than fifteen. That is despite or perhaps because of some interesting personal challenges. I have listed a few below.

Internal or external?

One of the unusual aspects of a career in program management is the fact that the role can be delivered by either a permanent employee or an external contractor. In no other part of corporate life is the difference as blurred as it is in this discipline.

This reflects a strange dynamic in transformation where the weight of external experience is considered far more highly than one's internal network or track record. One could almost say that the success of implementation is perceived to be dependent on whether the key delivery agent is internal or external!

We still live in a corporate world that attaches greater weight to experiences gained externally than to those who have invested in their career, network and internal relationships. Subject matter expertise within the precise organization that needs to go through a process of change is undervalued. While we live in a corporate environment where loyalty has considerably less currency that perhaps thirty or forty years ago, there is no doubt that the world of contracting and consulting carries considerably greater personal risk than a career that has been built internally.

Going external, then, is still more attractive, despite the perennial personal risk of unemployment and the fact that an internal role offers greater security.

Is choosing a program manager about the discipline or the individual?
In the minds of most management sponsors, not all program managers are the same. This reflects the need for careful selection in most areas of corporate life. However, the distinction is more marked within the program management discipline.

As an illustration, let me relate an opinion from a portfolio director of a large regional bank in Asia some years ago. His comment on the selection criteria was that the program would receive funding if the *right* program manager were assigned. In his opinion, that was as important as whether the project was aligned to any strategic rationale / direction. This reflects a lack of maturity in the discipline that needs to be addressed as the volume and complexity of the work continues to grow.

Defining characteristics
What are these people like? Are there any overriding characteristics that we can include in any hiring criteria? Would you recognize a program manager in the street?

David Heron, CEO of WBMS, a PE backed, fast growth executive search and interim solutions firm, is a good source of insight into those questions. David has spent almost twenty years in the world of recruitment and the last ten working with organizations going through some kind of transformation program. He has watched the rise of 'interim' placement from its early stages, and has seen some remarkable successes and a fair share of failures too.

David quotes one of his clients, a senior leader within the UK food retail world, following a major, successful transformation there.

'Process is vital, but personality is very important, too. We need to deliver things with humanity.'

The comment is powerful because it positions the 'human' alongside the deliverable focus. David looks back at the way leaders were perceived in the early stages of his career and notes an important change:

'When I think about leaders when I was growing up, they were normally very loud, shouted at you a lot. Quite dictatorial and very hierarchical.'

He describes his perception of successful program managers in contrast:

'But the people who are really successful at this work, they're humble individuals. They spend enormous amounts of time listening, but when they speak, people actually listen. They quietly go about doing their stuff. They often show some vulnerability. They're not interested in being the hero or getting a medal or a big bonus. They're motivated by doing the right thing.'

The ability to build a team

David's comments are a good segue into the other key component for successful transformation: the ability to assemble a team quickly, from different sources and with different corporate experiences. The characteristics of being a good listener, humility, and vulnerability are vital, not just in developing strong relationships, understanding culture and the ecosystem of the organization, but also deeply understanding the requirements. They really matter in the process of building a delivery team that is prepared to commit itself fully to the program. An anonymous quote from an interviewee below perhaps explains the issue most clearly:

'We had a goal, which was to find a new role for a successful delivery team and find other opportunities for them as a unit, but were ultimately unsuccessful. We did manage to move one of the key guys to another organization to deliver a program which was almost identical. The result was totally different...having led this incredibly successful program at our original client, he left after four weeks in the new place. They just had no idea how to set him up for success.'

Vulnerability and emotional commitment

John Monk spent his early career in the technology and telecom world before moving into the financial services sector in 2008, while based in Spain. Subsequently he built a career within one of the largest UK banking groups, program managing a number of divestments as the bank went through major global restructuring. The sector remains a highly process-oriented, male-dominated workplace. John was tasked with the sale of a small bank subsidiary in South America as part of the global restructuring. The moment arose when the employees of the business needed to be informed of the decision to sell the entity and of the impact on them and their employment. Their reaction was not something he had prepared for.

> 'I've never seen that level of emotion. I went back to my hotel room and had to really think about how to deal with this. And the answer was obvious. Be totally up front and honest, and roll my sleeves up and engage much more personally than I had ever done before. That was a real eye opener. And actually, very beneficial for me professionally. I learned a lot from that one.'

Some of the myths

Like all myths, most have a grain, and some have a truckload of truth about them.

The obsessive completer finisher myth

Chris Sykes is a program director with over twenty years' international experience, delivering major M&A integration programs around Asia and elsewhere. He captures the completer finisher requirement in a description of his interview with the CEO for one of the largest programs he had worked on:

> 'The Director who interviewed me for the job, I'd worked with him previously, his first question was "are you still anal?" I was a bit nonplussed by the question, but admitted that yes, I was still very detail oriented, if that was what he meant. His response was "good, that's exactly what I need."
>
> Ultimately the responsibility for delivery was on every one of the CEO's direct reports. It was a key performance indicator which we all had to work to. All of us were expected to own delivery.'

It is clear that being a completer finisher is not an unusual quality for a successful program manager. At its obsessive extreme, however, it becomes a hindrance to further progress.

Matthew Botelle has run some of the largest infrastructure programs in the UK and the Middle East. He has a fascination for railways and a real sense of the legacy that he has been responsible for developing.

His epiphany came when the program he was managing became so large that he couldn't retain the approximately 50,000 line plan in his head any more. He realized that in order to be successful he was going to have to select and trust those below him to manage parts of the program on his behalf. Typically, he chose some of the seemingly most awkward project managers, as their demeanor was indicative of their unwillingness to accept the status quo. This led them not only to have a detailed knowledge of delivery problems but also, given increased influence and authority, to take personal ownership in addressing them.

Change in a program...the inflection point

Some of the most fascinating parts of the interviews arose when I asked the interviewees about their own personal change as a result of their work experience. Sometimes we got to this part of the conversation with a classic retrospective 'What would you have done differently?' question. Often, however, the question that generated the most insightful commentary was about an inflection point.

In almost every program I've managed, there is a moment where something dramatic happens. Usually, the drama is not of the chair-throwing, "don't darken my doorstep" variety but something altogether more subtle.

John Monk's epiphany in the story about the South American bank was an inflection point: a moment when some of the basic premise on which a plan was built is discarded and needs to be reassembled in a very different way. It might be a moment when a senior stakeholder changes behavior in a really significant way, for example:

▸ The CEO of a major domestic telecom company stopped walking around the office and conducting meetings using classic financial management information, and instead spent three months with customer experience data, investigating, in some cases interrogating and often challenging his direct reports with the results that were apparent from that data.

▶ The moment when the CEO of a major wholesale banking division, who had never really stepped out of his office, and had certainly never had to manage people through change before, made a small step...literally. He came out of his office, went on to the dealing room floor, and struck up an informal conversation with people who had never had that experience before.

These moments are tattooed into the minds of program managers....and yet they don't exist in any project / program plan. They become a part of the shared and personal history of the team, and they change the way in which they work.

The microcosm of the program...or why do program managers do this work?

While there is much focus on the humility and self-effacing nature of program managers, there are some interesting other characteristics that talk to the need for control, structure, and ultimately authority.

Large transformation programs start to develop a life of their own. Their way of working develops in a way that is unique to the people within it. Unwritten rules are established over a period of time and provide some stability. Often these rules are different from the rest of the organization.

Certain behaviors develop within the program that are not possible in the 'business as usual' world. Examples might include the ability to make decisions quickly and revisit if they turn out to be the wrong ones. Situations where the best course of action after a mistake turns out to be to admit it, whereupon the team moves on. These mistakes provide an opportunity for the program team to reinforce their commitment to each other and their willingness to work together.

In a good program structure, there are other things that are stamped out as quickly and as early as possible. Being political in a tight, integrated structure ultimately comes across as being less than open and a bit dishonest. Those who try are often found out very early and tend to leave swiftly. Being unhelpful and unwilling to compromise and support are things that destroy the integrity of this little world. Those who do not help others find it a cold place, and often move on of their own accord.

Much of the motivation in doing this job comes from the excitement and challenge of engaging anew with a fellow group of travelers who have a commitment to the task ahead. It is an emotional commitment.

Ray Monaghan is someone every complex program needs. He comes from the world of systems development, and has spent his career delivering complex programs by being unashamedly rational and uncompromising in his approach. With that comes intellect, experience, clarity of thought around data, the effort required, and a focus on developing a single source of the truth. But at the heart of this mindset is also another perspective.

> 'Delivery or implementation is actually made up of what it's like to work with you, how the relationships are formed **and** what you actually deliver.
>
> When I started, because I was coming from a product implementation perspective, delivery was all about whether the product worked and whether it did all the things it needed to do within the budget.
>
> It wasn't really as much about the relationships. And that's probably where I've changed the most. These programs, they change people's lives. Spending two years on a program, that's a long time in your working life for the people in some of the organizations I've worked with. Making the experience of working on the program interesting and fun. I think that's something that people need to think about when they set the program up.
>
> There's an emotional commitment there. It's about a human commitment to the team and that creates some authenticity, some energy and ultimately the willingness to engage in it. I've worked on programs and projects where there was a huge amount of commitment in the team and it made a massive difference. You look back and think, could you have done what we did if everyone was a bit kind of halfhearted or just wanted to get out of the program? And the answer is no way. I've had people voluntarily working every hour of the day without being asked because they just were so committed to the

idea, they loved the solution, and they were so excited about delivering it for their company.'

When data is not really seen as 'data'

Whoever first came up with the concept, 'What gets measured gets done,' has created more problems than you can possibly imagine. The issue with that state-ment is that it inevitably draws you toward quantitative, numeric data points because that supposedly allows you to replicate, check, and test, and most impor-tantly analyze a trend.

It's a strange thing that qualitative data (that is, anecdotal / applied / sensory / story - based) is seen as a second-class citizen in the data family...and yet we as humans live as a consequence of our ability to understand this information in a nanosecond and respond at a speed that we ourselves are not aware of.

There are two fundamental issues with this concept:

First, the expectation of accuracy with regard to quantitative data does not stack up. For obvious reasons, the person I'm quoting below wants to remain anonymous. He is a very senior program delivery director and managing director steeped in the world of technology from the global investment banking sector.

'I've been involved long enough in the collection of that kind of data to know that to put it in the most positive light, it gets pushed to all sorts of different judgment calls before it's released externally to a third party or data market. By the time it gets out, it's been massaged to hell. If we're doing it, everybody else is doing it and yet the conclusions, when they come out the back end of that sausage machine, try to paint a picture of something very clean and very measurable. But our inputs aren't perfect because we don't have that knowl-edge to hand. At the end of the day, it's more than a pinch of salt. When you look at those conclusive statements about the state of market, the state of investment, when we've "lied," everybody else would've done the same thing and therefore how much can you rely on the information anyway?'

I recognize the controversial nature of the above statement. My interest is not whether published market data is accurate or not, but about the quality of the inputs. These illustrate the structural inefficiencies that exist within large businesses around the gathering of data.

Second, in several of my interviews the focus starts in the quantitative world but ends in the qualitative one, and indeed what is learned is almost always more about the experience of acting or not acting on qualitative data and not about better financial and management information analysis.

I do not draw a distinction between these sources of information, and I would ask you to do the same.

To conclude, there are a number of things to note about the program management community.

- Diversity. The people who manage programs for a living are incredibly broad in terms of demographics, race and gender, and industry background. The value of this diversity enables them to operate in a sector-agnostic manner. They are not bound by their previous experiences. Companies with a degree of program management maturity are increasingly attracted by this diversity of experience.
- Program managers have a skill set and capability that are as much defined by their emotional maturity and behavioral understanding as they are by any rational planning or stakeholder management knowledge. The latter is important, the former is critical!
- Their motivation is entrepreneurial in nature, albeit within the confines and structure of established organizations. The challenge of selecting, forming, developing teams, defining and iterating on the design of complex tasks, and leaving a legacy of a positive working experience plus a good result is at the heart of their ambition.

A note for anyone who is looking to develop their program management capability in-house. While it feels much easier to focus on the artefacts (tools that will help to create a consistent plan, reporting process, risk management system, dashboard, etc.), these are baubles that decorate rather than illuminate. Building a program management capability is fundamentally about building a team of people who have the emotional maturity and the right motivation and remain curious about the task ahead. Focus on the people, and you will end up with a function that can achieve remarkable things.

02
THE CASE STUDIES

Introduction

Occasionally you come across a transformation story that is remarkable. A story that raises the question: Is this a one-off, or are there really lessons for us all to learn as we travel on our own transformation journeys? In the course of my research, I have had the opportunity to hear some remarkable stories, which deserve a more in-depth description.

Why include case studies at all?
Case studies provide a complete picture of the transformation. They give a different set of perspectives based on those interviewed and their personal interpretation of the situation. There is little need for editorial input other than in the conclusion and a few other moments where it is valuable to take a step back and review the lessons. Good stories tell themselves.

Why these case studies?
For very different reasons, these three stories have a number of themes that make them particularly interesting.

▸ All three have a definitive period of transformation. This is important because it is possible to see cause and effect.
▸ In all three cases, the leadership team was new and had the benefit of operating from a blank sheet of paper. In two, the nature of the crisis the company faced forced a radically different approach and enabled seismic rather than incremental change. Perhaps this is a limitation in the context of a learning opportunity for those reading this. It is unusual not to have to consider an existing business

infrastructure in the course of delivering a transformation program. However, for anyone coming into a transformation program, there is a chance and often a requirement to build a team, change an approach, create a set of principles. All of these represent an opportunity for a fresh start for stakeholders and more importantly for the team members.

▸ In all three case studies, the scope of transformation encompassed the whole organization, not just a part of it. This holistic approach to change is interesting because it forced an approach which was as broad as it was deep. It was recognized that a small, precise intervention was not going to be enough. The program of change needed to empower others (beyond the leadership team) to interpret and implement as they felt appropriate. The role of leadership was not one of control but of guidance and an active relinquishing of decision making and ultimately power.

▸ All were delivered at pace.

What was the process of capturing these case studies?

In all cases, I heard these stories first-hand from senior leaders within the business. Subsequently I had the chance to talk to a number of others involved in the same organizations to get a different perspective and interpretation. In all cases, I interviewed them more than once to explore a specific part of the story in more detail. These secondary conversations were really valuable, and often led to a greater insight and understanding.

Why have I put them upfront?

The positioning of the case studies reflects the process I followed in writing this book. The framework that follows is an applied one based on the stories I have been told, rather than something dreamed up in a darkened room somewhere.

Nextel: A remarkable corporate recovery in Brazil

The announcement in March 2019 that Nextel was going to be bought by Mexico's America Movil for US$905m is perhaps a footnote during a period of frenetic M&A activity. It is, however, the end to a remarkable turnaround story. Twenty months before, the company had been sold to ANMT for US$200m in a fire sale. At this time, its future looked bleak.

Nextel Brazil was the fifth-largest telecom operator in Brazil, with a customer base in the major urban markets of Rio de Janeiro, Sao Paulo, and four other cities in Brazil, a market of around 30 million people.

The business was 'contract only' (not pre-pay), and had been successful in the Business to Business (B2B) marketplace. This was as a result of some proprietary 'Push to Talk' technology that Nextel owned, called iDEN. iDEN was in demand and in the early 2000s at the forefront of technological capability. With the advent of 3G, however, this technology was rapidly overtaken, and Nextel was very slow to respond. When they finally launched 3G, the offering had no differentiation to the bigger players in the market, and the company struggled to compete.

A changing sector

The downturn in Nextel's fortunes probably also reflected a change in the sector. Like many emerging markets, Brazil had experienced incredible growth in telco with a young, dynamic population looking for ever greater access to the Internet and the concomitant need for data. The sector responded to this opportunity. It was perceived as technology – focused, vibrant, innovative, and modern. Telco as a sector was able to leverage new technologies quickly and efficiently. It was close to its customers, resulting in a unique speed of response to consumer demand (very fast in comparison to other Business to Customer sectors).

In the 2010's, demand slowed. Expectations of continual innovation were replaced by a more exacting expectation of service, quality, and reduced cost. The sector struggled to adapt from a situation where growth was everything and cost control minimal to one where the reverse was the case. Telco companies found this change in focus difficult, perhaps a reflection of the fact that leadership had not changed at all in the same timeframe. In a period of less than twenty years, telecom operators had gone from leaders of innovation to businesses that were being challenged at every level.

This changing marketplace was reflected in the comparative fortunes of Nextel. With the advent of 3G and 4G in 2011 and the lack of adaption to that market by Nextel, the number of iDEN users fell from 4.1m to 0.3 million by 2017. The business was struggling operationally as well. Churn rates were in excess of 4.4%. Nextel found itself in a death spiral, with EBITDA (Earnings Before Interest Tax Depreciation and Amortization) losses of Brazilian Real 207m, impending debt repayments of Brazilian Real 752m (within eighteen months) and very limited cash. The business had less than six months to turn itself around.

The share price reflected this change. Between July 2015 and April 2017, the company's NASDAQ listed share price fell thirty-nine times from a high of US$14.30 to a low point of US$0.37.

Which customer?....making the right decision

As a telecom market, Brazil has some interesting and unique characteristics when it comes to customer engagement. In an early survey done by Nextel one of the findings was that most customers (over 70%) knew which mobile operator their friends were using. Service and performance levels appeared to be topics that were discussed regularly and frequently.

As with most telecom operators, making decisions about which customer segment to focus on had never been a strong point. In Nextel's case, of the six potential segments they were servicing across both Business to Business (B2B) and Business to Customer (B2C), only one was making any money and showing some potential for growth.

For most of the rest, in particular within the B2B world, performance was awful. Customer acquisition costs were in the top 10% compared with the rest of the market. A key telco measure, the average revenue per user (ARPU) was lower than anyone else in the domestic B2C sector, and that did not include the fact that the company was giving some handset subsidies. Customer conversion rates were poor, perhaps a blessing in disguise given the loss-making profile of this sub-sector. Growth, in other words, was nonexistent.

A change in leadership

Remote shareholders often struggle with an appropriate speed of response to changing market conditions. For Nextel's shareholders, the impending disaster had been highlighted a number of months before. After some delay, the decision was made to replace the CEO and a short-list of two was drawn up.

Roberto Rittes perceived himself as the underdog. In many ways, his career to that date encapsulated everything that a large US shareholder might have wanted. Roberto started his career with UBS, one of the largest investment banks with a focus on the Telecom, Media, and Technology sectors, specifically within Latin America. He had done an MBA at Harvard before cutting his teeth with one of the largest telecom providers, Brasil Telecom. He had had some experience with private equity, initially looking for transactions before joining a portfolio company as a Board Member.

This, however, was his first pitch for a CEO role. It was a pitch for a role with a company that, without major surgery, would have only a few months to live. His pitch was challenging. What Roberto was suggesting was not just the typical deep cost-cutting process that was a familiar well-trodden path for crisis remediation. He was also talking about short- to medium-term growth, a concept that had proven elusive for previous leadership. In his view, cutting costs was very important and would buy the company some time, but it was not going to be enough. To their credit, the shareholders decided that Roberto was the right choice.

What comes first? Cost reduction, growth, or what?

What Roberto had highlighted in his pitch was the challenge of cost reduction versus growth. Typically, one of the challenges for any major restructuring process is that taking cost out has a detrimental impact on any growth opportunity. Ultimately growth is driven by the willingness of employees to take some personal risks in the form of new ideas around operational improvement, or innovation, or customer service. If all around them they see redundancy and cost reduction, the likelihood of putting their heads above the parapet and suggesting these types of ideas is going to be very low.

Roberto and his leadership team had therefore to tread a very fine line between fear (caused by major cost reduction and resulting in 'flight' or 'freeze') and encouragement. Furthermore, he was unknown in the marketplace and was replacing a high-profile leader. The level of skepticism internally as to whether he would succeed was high.

His first step was to change the pace of the organizaton. Speed of thought, speed of decision making, energy, and enthusiasm became his main focus. Within a few weeks of arriving, he had fired a whole layer of his direct reports. In his assessment, there were people below them who had the capability and drive to do the roles well, and through this action he was delivering a very powerful message to the organization at large. 'Performance management' was going to start at the top of the organization, not the bottom. In our discussion, he commented, 'When you get rid of a layer, especially one at the top of the organization, people get excited, they get promoted. It's a positive agenda and demonstrates immediately that we're going to be changing this business.'

Building a leadership team

Bringing in a new team had an immediate impact on the organization. It was the first time that many of the team would take on leadership responsibility. While there were some external appointments, around 60% of the new leadership team came from within the business. Two other key characters became central to the transformation.

Pedro Arakawa was the first to join. Pedro was running Customer Care, but was promoted to chief commercial officer, running Sales, Marketing, Customer Care, and Customer Operations. Pedro mirrored Roberto's energy and enthusiasm, but also challenged his colleagues in terms of the level of innovation and pace.

The second person was Marcelo Amar, head of Information Technology. Marcelo provided a balance in terms of calm, pragmatic assurance to the team. In the telco sector transformation in technology is extremely challenging, given the number of moving parts and the requirements of changing systems while maintaining an active service. Marcelo provided a level of maturity and insight that made him an enabler for change rather than someone who blocked it.

Alongside this inner group, there were a number of other key advisers. David Cox was a senior customer experience specialist, having worked around the world building customer experience capability in the sector for more than twenty years. David was engaged early on in the transformation program, and provided the customer analytics and experience insight that drove many of the initiatives. He describes the key challenges from a customer experience perspective:

> 'The first step is to very simply stop pissing your customers off. I know that sounds really basic and really obvious. Perhaps that why it's often overlooked. Doing that early allows the organization to cut through all of the noise and to listen very clearly. It doesn't need us trying to do anything clever. It just needs us to listen to customers telling us what is going wrong in detail so that we can fix it.'

Maintaining the energy and providing clarity of purpose

Over the next six months, the organization reduced its workforce by 30%. Despite this, in the period from April 2017 to January 2018, the Net Promotor Score jumped from around +13 to +30. (Net Promotor Score, or NPS, is the most established and effective way of measuring employee engagement. It has a simple question at its core: 'Would you recommend this company to your family and friends?'). This would be a remarkable uplift in a steady-state environment, let alone one going through this level of restructuring.

What was core to this success was a balance between cutting costs and improving the customer experience. From day one, the message was clear: 'We are going to fix churn by creating the best customer experience in the industry.' Within ten days of starting, Roberto had commenced a project aimed at reducing churn and hired some external support to help him with this.

In the first two months of the churn project, the business was losing 60,000-70,000 clients per month. Six months later, Nextel was gaining clients per month. While this was clearly a key to financial stability, it also provided a welcome distraction from the cost reduction agenda. Most importantly, it was a live demonstration that what they were doing was working.

The organization had gone from a trajectory of closing within four months to being the fastest growing telecoms provider in Brazil. They achieved this within two years, with 10% of the marketing spend of any of their competitors.

What's really interesting about Nextel's story is that there is no attempt to disguise the complexity of the process. Reducing customer acquisition costs, improving customer service, selling more, changing the perception of the brand...none of these are simple processes, and none of them were processes that any competitor was going through. There was no external benchmark against which to test success.

Each of these major initiatives had implementation challenges, and as Roberto described it, it became very easy to identify who the 'doers' were. In his definition, these were people who could manage the internal roadblocks, eliminating them or navigating around them. Those who couldn't either left or were sidelined.

Changing the culture

The legacy

Previous management had adopted a 'command and control' style that had created a highly compliant, but not particularly engaged workforce. This was perhaps also part of the 'big' company legacy, with bloated support functions, highly siloed ways of working, and lots of bureaucratic procedures / processes. There was a core group of employees who had been at Nextel for more than eight years through the growth period. There was no sense that change was required, and no real experience of how to bring this about.

With the change of leadership, a change of culture followed very quickly.

...taking layers out

Reducing layers in a business has a cultural impact as well as a financial one. It forces leadership to push decision making down in the organization, giving those closest to the decision the autonomy to make it.

Roberto and his team moved from the traditional annual planning process to a quarterly update, setting priorities, providing data, and reconfirming overall direction (the 'North' as he describes it). This led to teams' responding quickly and proactively.

...changing working practices, starting with communication

Roberto's own management style became a critical factor in changing culture. His focus on internal communications led to a schedule which included around fifteen ninety-minute monthly meetings with different parts of the business, connecting with employees at every level. He was also running at least one employee meeting per week as a source of feedback and insight.

During these meetings, the operational challenges and performance of the business was discussed with complete openness and honesty. There was never any attempt to sugarcoat the results. This approach permeated throughout the organization.

....self-selection for key initiatives

The process of identifying those with the right approach became important as the number of key initiatives in its transformation agenda grew. This was as much about attitude and desire as it was about capability. It became very easy to identify those team members who were excited by the possibility of doing something new and innovative, challenging themselves and those around them. By contrast, those who were looking for excuses as to why these initiatives were not going to work also stood out. The strategy of identifying people who were excited by the change agenda was adopted by his direct reports and their teams very quickly. The process of self-selection also helped to reduce headcount further as the organization began to move through the implementation phase and build momentum.

...measuring what worked and what didn't with the customer and allocating ownership

The core customer experience program provided a structured tracking system which gave continuous updates as to what was and what was not working. The tracking system also provided a platform for regular customer engagement. The organization recognized the value of quantitative data through the tracking process and also the power of qualitative data. Teams were encouraged to share stories and experiences in every forum.

David Cox identifies a key moment of engagement when different parts of the customer experience journey were allocated directly to senior leaders. This was not a 'sponsor' role with some kind of non-executive responsibility. It was direct and personal ownership. David comments:

'What that [executive ownership] does is get you to the point where you have somebody who owns a moment in the journey and you're able to tell her very directly that 37% of your customers are fed up at that particular moment. That's ugly. It's painful. It causes people to sweat. What you create is this change of mindset where the focus is on the customer and what they're telling us. That then works back through into your own internal KPIs [key performance indicators] and all the usual stuff that people are used to measuring and managing. We're turning that customer feedback into one of those KPIs.'

...measuring performance internally with a change in HR policies and metrics

Performance at Nextel had always been measured through key performance indicators, or KPIs. These were focused on 'business as usual' performance and driven by activity rather than outcome. The achievement of these KPIs had a direct impact on bonus.

At Nextel in 2017, the ratio of personal to corporate KPIs was 70:30. In other words, a number of managers were exceeding personal KPI targets that were often poorly designed, while the organization as a whole was in a death spiral. They were due a bonus while the business failed.

• An early example of this practice was the conversion of paper invoices to e-billing. This was a specific KPI for an individual who had taken the arbitrary decision to migrate 300,000, 10% of the total customer base, to e-billing without *any* communication with the customers affected. The immediate result was a big spike in bad debts, driven by email addresses that were no longer correct, and no warning, so that customers were not prepared for the change. The negative impact on customer feedback was tangible.

Within six weeks of the start of the transformation program, this balance was reversed to 30% personal / team, 70% company KPIs.

In the following year, Roberto and his team also introduced the concept of Objectives and Key Results (OKRs).

OKRs are a simple, binary, outcome-based measurement concept with a couple of simple measures (key results) showing progress along the way. Ultimately an OKR asks a simple question: 'Did we do it or did we not?,' which is very appropriate for organizations being run on program management based principles. The shift to OKRs also enabled the payment of bonuses based on individuals' specific deliverables and behaviors (the 'how' as well as the 'what').

Performance measurement became an active tool for leadership. Further changes were introduced in 2019 to reflect the need for a change in the balance between delivering new initiatives and maintaining the existing business. Up until that moment the focus had been on the new. However, with performance improving, business maintenance became important again. The organization ended up with a hybrid model that included both outcome-based and activity-based measurement.

What is really interesting about this change is the creation of a business and corporate culture that could move quickly and relatively seamlessly between change and business as usual, to reflect the demands of the customer base and the changes within the industry. This constant rebalancing ability while not losing the trust of employees is something that many organizations strive toward but very few achieve.

Changing direction...becoming an outcome-focused business.

What is fascinating about Roberto's approach is that he is moving his entire organization away from 'business as usual' mode and into a shape that has some core program and project management disciplines at its heart. Pushing decision making and accountability down to the most appropriate level, communicating constantly and authentically, actively selecting people who can execute and implement with minimal direction, building collaboration through engagement... these are all classic techniques in delivering complex programs, and they become the modus operandi for Nextel.

The above change also starts to create a perfect employee engagement process, based on actions and deliverables. Nextel started measuring employee NPS in 2017, based on the understanding that happy clients were a mirror of a happy and engaged team. In less than two years they reduced employee detractors from 40% to 5%.

How?

- ▸ Providing open, honest, and clear communication about the state of the business, its challenges, and its opportunities.
- ▸ Using a range of communications channels to address the organization in the most effective way.
- ▸ Removing layers of bureaucracy, demonstrating decisiveness, and being open to ideas, irrespective of position and experience.
- ▸ Operating at speed and giving autonomy to those with capability.

All the above lends itself to the 'remedial' nature of the situation. Creating cohesion and commitment is often easier when survival is in doubt. An external threat provides a powerful backdrop or context against which to change things at pace. If that threat potentially impacts those with whom one feels a connection or a closeness, the sense of responsibility and cohesion grows even stronger. In my Nextel interviews, the word that was used the most when describing the culture was 'family'. There was a depth to employees' relationships. There was a sense of purpose that what they were doing was important.

Another critical element of changing the employees' relationship with the organization was to give them an external focus, something they could believe in and engage with, and to let them see that their actions were having a positive impact on people's lives. This is where the Nextel Customer concept became a key component of the transformation program.

The Nextel Customer

It is a little counterintuitive to focus on a customer group with the least disposable income and perhaps the least potential from which to grow revenues. Servicing the working poor is not a strategy that many companies adopt willingly, given the choice. That is reflected in that segment's customer experience, which is usually horrific.

In Rio de Janeiro, Sao Paolo, and the other larger cities in Brazil, the working lives of this group of customers is challenging. They tend to live in or around neighborhoods on the outskirts of the city, with three to four hours' commute every day. Each salary earner will have two or three dependants. They are usually degree qualified, working as sales agents, drivers, or small shop entrepreneurs. They are time-poor and highly dependent on their cell phones in work and for communication with their families. David Cox describes this customer base in the context of the customer experience journey:

> 'Once we'd done the basics [around where things go wrong], we started to build in the positive. And this is where the story really starts to become interesting. The process first of all is to understand what really matters to your customers. The question is not "What do you want?" The question is "What matters to you? What really matters in your life?"
>
> We started to home in on a segment of the population who had an affinity with us as an organization. We called the segment the hardworking man / woman. Sao Paulo is a really hard city, and these guys live a really tough life. They live out in the suburbs. They travel two hours to work every day. They don't get paid very much. It's a pretty grim life. They are the forgotten people in the city. Nobody gives a shit about them. And, most importantly, nobody is their champion. But like the rest of us, these people have hopes and dreams. They want a better life, and so on. What we did was to create an identity, an essence, a purpose, which was based squarely on creating opportunity for these people. Nextel went from being an operator that provides Internet on your phone to being a business that put ourselves firmly in their lives, with a mission to make their lives easier.'

For this group of customers, the ambition to create the best possible customer experience in the marketplace had enormous psychological value. It led directly to extraordinary levels of loyalty, trust, and growth. It also became one of the key drivers for employee engagement. Looking at the internal and external messaging, that alignment becomes really clear. This is how Nextel described its purpose:

> 'Nextel believes that everyone deserves to succeed in life. But we know that's not easy for everyone, especially for the hard-working everyday heroes. And we respect that. We are fair, we come clean, we find solutions fast. We get straight to the point. We understand and deliver what they need. Because tomorrow the battle continues, and we're on the same side. That's why we're not afraid to go further. When everyone says we can't, we just do it – more than delivering,

We make things happen straight away.

This is our purpose: to make every customer's life easier so that tomorrow will be better than today.'

An identity with a purpose...going local

The decision to become a local telecom operator, working from within the neighbor-hoods where the customers are based, was a pragmatic one. Reducing the portfolio of centrally located retail stores was easier than selling those in the outskirts and was linked with the customer strategy.

Maintaining a local presence became an opportunity to reinforce that profile. As is typical for a business with the appetite for change, all sorts of things were tried out and succeeded or failed:

▸ Using the local stores on the weekends to teach graffiti art to locals was a power-ful reminder of Nextel's commitment to the neighborhood.
▸ Supporting the local university football teams, in direct contrast to the national team branding and sponsorship by the largest telecom provider, Vivo, was less of a success. Despite much effort, the lack of a well-run league, the intricacies of existing ownership and sponsorship structures and the local university gover-nance structures in the end killed what looked like a powerful initiative.

A product that was not 'fit for purpose'

The Brazilian telco sector struggled with an abundance of different offers, plans, needs, and customer requirements, which led to a confusing product. The drivers for this confusion were as much down to the local regulator as a basic misunder-standing of customer needs. Complexity made comparison difficult, which had been perceived as an advantage. With the evolution of other fixed-rate subscription services (Spotify, Netflix), the market needed to change. The operators started to understand that simplicity of product was a better strategy.

In 2017, Nextel was in the worst of all places from a customer experience perspec-tive. They offered more than ten plans that looked simple but in reality contained a number of hidden charges:

- The company made significant income (up to 10% of Average Revenue Per User or ARPU) from very expensive SMS-based subscription services. These offered very little value to the consumer and created a lot of customer dissatisfaction.
- Of the plans on offer, none made any obvious mention of the price of long-distance calls. In Brazil, thirty minutes out of a major city would be categorized as long-distance, and for many customers, with a commute from outside the city into their place of work, that was a daily occurrence.
- The consequence was that monthly charges were often 20-30% higher than the advertised price, creating significant 'Bill shock' for the customer. 80% of the 70,000 calls to the call center to April 2017 were described as regarding bill dispute.

Simplification creates trust

Simplifying a service offering or product sends a very powerful message to the customer. It says, 'We believe that what we offer has value,' 'We believe that what we charge is reasonable and appropriate,' and 'We value our relationship with you enough to be entirely open and transparent about our charges.'

In late 2017, Nextel decided to take a typically radical approach to this simplification challenge. The company went from ten to three plans in total, with the only variable being the amount of data. Everything else (Voice / SMS) was unlimited. The company also cut a large part of the additional 'valued added' services sold. For those that remained, Nextel changed the buying process to a 'double opt-in' methodology. This was a major contributor in cutting the number of customer disputes by 90% in three months.

Migrating customers to the new plans was the next challenge. This is a process that typically takes a long time, given customers' adversity to change. From a commercial perspective, the temptation is also to drag the migration process out. The telecom operator tends to take an ARPU hit with migration. In Nextel's case, they decided to drive conversion as fast as possible. Over a seven-month period, the company managed to migrate 93% of all customer plans to the new unlimited plans. Customer disputes overall fell by more than 41% over the same period (with calls regarding billing falling by 61%).

Managing the transformation program

It's easy to imagine that the journey that Nextel went through was developed at a strategic level with a set of detailed plans, breaking each long-term initiative down into a series of activities by function, timeline, and allocated resource. That is, after all, the classic top–down approach that many transformation programs follow.

At Nextel, the approach was different. The organization worked to four distinct objectives:

1. 'All-in as a Customer Centric Company.' The definition of this was: 'It doesn't even look like telecom: all-in to serve clients better at every point of contact.'
2. 'Disruptive mindset to deliver higher growth.' This was defined as 'leveraging attacker marketing position and rapid implementation of new low cost channels to accelerate growth while reducing sales and marketing costs.'
3. Cost Leadership to deliver solid EBITDA. This was described as 'using traditional and digital tools to squeeze every possible drop of cost out of our business.'
4. Agile and lean culture and organization. The definition of this objective was to 'Quickly adopt new economy management tools, practices, and operating model to engage employees and accelerate decision making and execution.'

None of these are remarkable statements. They are not particularly ear-catching in terms of the language used. They are not innovative as concepts. In some cases, the combination of objectives feels a little clunky. Some of them use 'emotional' language. All of them could probably find their way into many organizations' objectives, and most of them could be expressed more succinctly or with greater impact.

Why, then, did these become so important in managing this program? The answer seems remarkably simple, and falls into four easy ideas:

1. Executive ownership.
2. Short-time horizons.
3. Close measurement.
4. A willingness to consider every idea with a ruthlessness to discard those that don't work quickly.

What were the practical steps that enabled this to work?

1. There was no strategic annual plan. Instead, leadership and the teams agreed on a limit of ten projects to deliver within the next quarter, on a quarter-by-quarter basis.
2. The projects were set up in part with 'agile' methodology including two-week sprints, fail-fast decision making, etc. However, there were two variants from this approach:

    i.   There was an executive owner. There is a distinction here between 'sponsorship' and 'ownership.' The former often translates as oversight and 'arm's length' to the delivery effort, while the latter means accountability and day-to-day engagement in implementation. Direct ownership created urgency at the most senior level in the organization.
    ii. The selection process for those to manage the projects was rigorous. It became clear that there was a special skill set required, and the business actively sought these skills from among the employee base.

3. The teams for each project sat together physically for the quarter.
4. The question asked for each project changed from 'What are we going to do?' to 'What is the result that we need to achieve?' This created a powerful link between outcome and benefit, and is where the cultural transformation began. Nextel became a project-based organization.
5. Quarterly time frames created time pressure and the need for immediate action. There was no time for long definition processes, market and competitor analysis, and detailed planning.

Engagement and customer feedback needed to be immediate and continuous. The whole organization was involved, irrespective of function and seniority.

1. Measurement. In order to measure things accurately, you needed to know what you were looking for. Finding innovative ways to identify whether you were achieving this outcome required collaboration. The organization quickly recognized that good ideas could come from anywhere. It also recognized that no one could actually predict what was going to work and therefore the only thing that mattered was the ability to start and stop quickly.

David Cox, who was responsible for Customer Experience and a key architect and driver behind the transformation program, describes the change in the organization:

> 'The organization became so tight. We moved away from departmental initia-tives, fifty-seven things to do and everyone clashing. Suddenly there were only ten projects, that was it. How to achieve the result was entirely up to the owner...all management cared about was the "what." There was a direct line between the "north star" and the people working on the activities themselves.'

The program in action....some examples of success

One of the main targets that Roberto brought from his previous experience was to develop digital marketing into a proper sales channel. He and his team identified that the time taken between the initial interest and follow-up was critical if you wanted to improve customer conversion rates. In April 2017 it took typically two to three days to follow up after initial interest. By June 2017, and with focus and a new process, they were able to move this to one to two minutes from initial interest.

While this was in itself remarkable, the team wanted more. This led to a need to change the sales system. Processing a new sale was taking twenty minutes—far too long for both customers and sales agents. By reviewing and drastically reduc-ing the amount of information required, they were able to reduce this to six to seven minutes.

The next part of the puzzle was SIM card delivery. In the past, using a traditional supply chain structure with a centralized warehouse, delivering a SIM card to a new customer would take up to a week. This had a significant negative impact on conversion rates. The solution the organization came up with was aligned with the local, neighborhood-based branding of Nextel. Initially each of the local shops was converted into a mini warehouse for SIM. Delivery times were good, but costs were high as motorcycle delivery agents had to go back to these warehouses to pick a SIM card and its 'mandatory invoice.' The decision was made to deliver SIM cards free (charging through the activation fee), eliminating the need to pick up the invoice. This enabled delivery agents to start the day with a bag full of SIM cards and make continuous deliveries within their territory. Same day delivery initially cost three times as much, but with the new model and delivery management software the cost was reduced so successfully that in the end it was 20% lower than the traditional centralized model. Nextel had moved from a process that might take seven days to one where 75% of SIM cards were delivered within two hours of sign-up. This single step reduced cancellations by 15%.

To summarize, a process that used to take nine to ten days from enquiry to completion was now being completed in two to four hours.

What is really interesting about this story is how 'human' the transformation discovery process is. You can imagine the slightly chaotic workshop in which the process is developed. It starts with some structure, perhaps a high-level ambition, a clear sense of who the customer is and what they need, and some focus on an aspect of the business where performance is poor. This is led by the CEO and perhaps someone focused on customer experience.

After that, however, a series of discussions starts to take place, each of which begins to unravel the cause of this poor performance and tries to develop a solution. All the dynamics of human discovery are visible...a myriad ideas, the tendency to go into rabbit holes, someone in the group looking to bring the discussion back to a practical level, a sudden inflection point, perhaps by someone sitting in the corner who has been listening and not necessarily contributing to the discussion.

Each solution uncovers another problem, which in turn is again resolved through a pragmatic, task-oriented, open-minded way of operating. The process is entirely organic, incremental, and iterative, and it leads to a result that would have been inconceivable at the start. The impact on customer perception is dramatic and memorable. The employees' belief in their abilities to solve complex, difficult problems grows and becomes self-perpetuating.

An early target was to reduce the cost to acquire customers, at the time running at approximately USD110 per customer. This included marketing costs, commissions paid to salespeople, and all the operational costs incurred. Within two quarters, the number had been reduced to USD79, a 26% reduction against a stretch target of USD57.

At the same time, churn needed to be addressed. In July 2017, this was running at 4%, a level that meant they were losing between 60,000 and 70,000 customers per month. By the end of 2017, this had been reduced to 2.5%.

It is worth considering these two examples in a bit of detail. There are two things that were particularly interesting and innovative about Nextel's approach.

- First, the improvements were not based on some external industry benchmark. They were based on an internal perspective that challenged the result in a holistic way. In effect, an expectation was being set out with the narrative 'whatever has gone before or happens elsewhere doesn't work in our company.'
- Second, by giving the project that kind of stretch target there was no possibility that the organization could achieve it by tinkering at the edges. It needed a complete change, in which all aspects of the process had to be challenged. This reduced the possibility of the classic change killer, 'We've tried it before and it didn't work,' being activated.

The results

Throughout this story I've provided some key results concerning financial performance and customer metrics. These have included business growth, customer churn, the cost to acquire and plan migration, and some employee engagement figures, in particular net promoter score (NPS).

The trouble with reporting these types of numbers is that first, they do not really demonstrate the extraordinary turnaround that Roberto and his team achieved, and second, all the success looks linear, when the reality is much more complex.

It is also easy to look at each individual dimension in isolation, understand the actions, and underestimate the effort and the innovation required to achieve the change.

The story is not simple:

- It is not just a story of bringing a new leadership team, firing the old and cutting costs to the bone.
- It is not a story of actively managing customer experience and building an

extraordinary offering in a market where the competitor base was static and vulnerable.
- It is not a story of finding some magic new disruptive technology that changes the marketplace and provides a new buying focus for customers.
- It is not a story of a massive capital injection, either through the acquisition of a complementary organization that provides the skill set and existing customer base to leverage, or by the dedication of resource to the internal development of something new.

There is no silver bullet here!

Instead, there are a number of intangible and qualitative actions that combine to release the extraordinary capability and innovation of a collective group of people.

What are those actions?

- A clear, unadulterated, and very personal sense of purpose, matched by a transformation process that engages the entire organization.
- A cultural shift where energy, passion, and drive replace complacency, fear of failure, and blame.
- Openness and honesty in terms of employee and customer communications. An extraordinary dedication to this effort in terms of communications channel selection and time.
- Decisiveness and personal accountability at all levels.

Above all, what makes Nextel unique is its ability to continuously balance its effort between change and 'business as usual,' between traditional telecom operator and digital services provider, between tight quantitative performance measurement and highly intuitive qualitative feedback.

It is easy to look at Nextel as a transformation case study with a series of neat, well defined, small, incremental programs. The real story, however, lies in the collective nature of what was achieved....in the whole, not the parts.

Postscript

I recently had the opportunity to speak with one of the architects of the Nextel story, Pedro Arakawa. My particular interest in talking to him was to understand what had happened in the intervening period, specifically in 2019, when the business was sold. Did the organization have some resilience, especially in the light of the impending insecurity that a change of control was bound to create among the employee base?

By way of context and in preparation for sale, the focus for 2019 was to bolster EBITDA and preserve cash. The impact on network performance was negative, as all continuous development requirements were halted. Anything that was not critical in terms of investment was postponed until after the sale to maximize value.

Pedro's response was unequivocal. The business maintained many of the same attributes, despite a change in leadership and the focus on sale. The employee base remained highly motivated, which maintained brand and customer focus. In the calendar year of 2019, customers grew from 3.2 million to 3.5 million.

The London Olympics in 2012: Complex infrastructure in the financial crisis

History

> 'The project management around an Olympic Games is of an inordinate complexity. No city is ever challenged under normal circumstances in a way that a city is challenged to deliver an Olympic and Paralympic games.'
> (Sebastian Coe, BBC Radio 4, The Reunion)

In terms of complexity, there's probably not much more challenging than hosting an Olympic Games. The stakeholder management requirement on its own provides significant challenge without considering the other dimensions of time pressure, the level of scrutiny around public spending on this scale, and the global and local attention of media and other interested parties.

When, in July 2005, it was announced that London had won the chance to host the Olympics in 2012 against a strong and highly regarded bid from Paris, the reaction from both the public and government was ecstatic. Tony Blair famously described it as a 'momentous day.' Lord Coe, Chairman of the London Organising Committee for the Olympic and Paralympic Games (LOCOG), called it 'the most fantastic opportunity to do everything we ever dreamed of in British sport.'

It did not take long, however, for the euphoria to die down. It was perhaps unfortunate but inevitable that comparisons with the redevelopment of Wembley Stadium were going to be made. Wembley was finally delivered at a cost of £757 million, more than double the original estimate and five years later than planned.

Added to that, the London Olympics, perhaps uniquely, was won three years prior to the financial crisis of 2008/9. The pressure on public spending and the focus on 'vanity' projects was probably never greater, and the impact on 'flexible' aspects of the budget was considerable.

Addressing this issue in an interview in 2009, David Higgins, CEO of LOCOG, was clear on how to respond. He commented:

'People will say, in tough times, is this a frivolous project? Are you sure that you are not wasting money? Is this a few weeks of party or is it really long-term investment? We need to show that we are competent and that we've thought through that what we are delivering has a long-term benefit for the city.' (New Civil Engineer, 6th January 2009)

In 2009, two years into the program, the value of this level of financial focus became really clear. The budget was intact, with around 25% spent and a number of decisions made that were going to be important in managing costs going forward. Acknowledging the challenge, he commented:

'We can't solve the credit crunch but we can competently manage the project – that is within our control.' (New Civil Engineer, January 6, 2009)

Complex?

From a top-down perspective, time pressures, international focus, and budget challenges for an Olympic Games creates a picture of complexity that would make most program managers quake a little. If you cut it down to its bare bones, however, the causes of that complexity are not so obvious.

▸ Building a stadium that can seat 80,000-100,000 people is not unique, and there was plenty of experience, domestically and internationally. Equally so for an aquatic center or a velodrome.

▸ Managing the infrastructure in a city like London was always going to be difficult for the people attending, if less so for the participants. No doubt there is more complexity in an older city that is struggling to adapt to the needs of modern life. As the organizers discovered and perhaps anticipated, the possibility of coming up with solutions that were really impactful was going to be unlikely. This was a case for managing existing transport solutions as effectively as possible—not easy, but hardly complex.

▸ Dealing with a mixed-use, part-industrial, brownfield site had some serious challenges, in particular with regard to what to do with the waste. One of these challenges was the limited diligence that had been conducted prior to bid. In discovery, the condition of the site from an environmental perspective was significantly worse than had been anticipated. With the green agenda being part of the winning formula and in the context of the budget available, the simple solution (landfill) was neither possible nor desirable. Ultimately the strategic solution was simple, even if the implementation was ingenious and, at the time, a global first for something of that scale.

So, if not in the scope of work, where then does the root cause of complexity lie?

Stakeholders...lots of them

Stakeholder management for an event such as the Olympics is a remarkable process. It is a feat just to capture the different interested parties and understand how they interact with the decision-making bodies of the games.

Producing a diagram or chart can be useful here, not least in drawing people together to understand where they fit into the process.

For the program managers within LOCOG, it was necessary to build a communications framework in the form of a diagram that clarified why certain groups of stakeholders would receive information first, and others later. Their diagram provided a graphic context of the complexity of communications, and showed how different groups fitted into different parts of the program. It also answered a number of important questions:

- ▸ Why it was necessary to have such a gradient of communications.
- ▸ Why certain groups were less important than others.
- ▸ Why the communications effort would have to shift its focus at certain stages in the program. Specifically, from the design phase, where the individual international sports authorities were important to engage (to ensure compliance against required sporting standards), to implementation, where their input was less important.

The other dimension around the communications plan was an understanding of channels, specifically which would be the most appropriate and most impactful channel in which situation. A good example of this arose with the engagement process for the local community. For this group, the impact of a major building program on their daily lives was particularly acute, in terms of both traffic and noise.

It became clear early on that in order to engage with the local community, town halls and traditional meetings were not going to be enough. As a consequence, LOCOG began a series of monthly visits in which groups were taken around the main stadium site in mini-buses with a guide to explain the stages in development, key challenges, and the approach being taken. This represented a significant problem for the contractors, specifically around health and safety, but was important in maintaining a positive link to the local community and the legacy use of the site.

There are stakeholders....and stakeholders – different motivations and perceptions of risk

The Olympic Delivery Authority (ODA, the body charged with developing the site to hand over to the LOCOG) was a brand new, special-purpose vehicle. Employees were aware that their contract was for the period of the build alone, or seven years. Their decision to join LOCOG was based on the unique experience it would give them, existing relationships, and all the other reasons that are relevant in any employment decision.

The decision for the employees of other stakeholder bodies, like the Greater London Authority (GLA), however, was different. For them, the Olympics represented a change to their working lives, more pressure, uncertainty, and a challenging legacy that would be theirs to manage and maintain. The nature of governance and decision making in these organizations was based on a pace and a process that was not fit for purpose for a program of this size and scale. This was reflected in the level of program management maturity and experience.

Creating a 'way of working' with or across these groups was going to be challenging and time consuming.

Aligning stakeholders

The process of managing change requests in any program of complexity is challenging. For stakeholders outside the program, it feels like a relatively boring, bureaucratic process that adds little value and needs little focus. The reality, however, is that the process is core to delivery and has an important role to play to have any chance of delivering the program within budget.

In a building program, the cost of managing change poorly becomes blinding obvious as the workers on site stop work and wait for the change in scope to be agreed. It is the perfect way to lose control of the budget.

Very early in the London Olympics 2012 program, four tightly grouped decision points were set. They represented stages of approval, and their purpose was threefold:

1. Each decision point enabled the release of a small amount of budget to take the design further. The tight timeline enabled iteration, but in a very controlled manner.
2. Each decision point served as an opportunity to bring key stakeholders together to discuss and agree on changes, voice concerns, and debate design options.
3. Each decision point provided another opportunity for familiarity and engagement.

This additional process was fundamental in one key aspect of control. It enabled the leadership team to limit the potential for scope change in the later part of the program. This is typically when costs and overruns escalate. Challenging scope later in a process becomes more difficult to justify if you have been involved in the design and have had at least four opportunities to comment and amend.

This was an important theme in implementation. The leadership team quickly adopted the 'defending the scope with your lives' core principle in the program. This was supported by some other techniques that made challenge difficult. An example of this was how the scope was presented.

▸ On completion of the scoping process, post Full Business Case Approval, the program of work was professionally printed and bound in its entirety. It was the size of an old phone book, and became known as 'The Yellow Book' because of the color of its cover. I am told that those copies that still exist are guarded closely. The purpose was clearly not to create a memento (!) but to make challenge more difficult. It is much harder to challenge something beautifully produced than something altogether more temporary in appearance.

This approach to written communication was used throughout the program to great effect. Materials that had a communications role were edited, illustrated, and printed with great care.

Solving the age-old problem of 'amateur' sponsors and 'professional' contractors. The advent of delivery partners

Managing the contractors...the context
From time immemorial, the process of managing government-financed building programs had been based on an unequal relationship.

‣ Funding was in the hands of experienced bureaucrats who were in positions of power because of their ability to manage government departments. This position was unrelated to their ability to understand and manage complex, multiyear building programs.
‣ To maintain checks and balances behind the release of funds, the usual approach was to divide the budget into various parts, and individual departments owned these independently of each other. While the treasury was the final arbiter, the process of spending approval was long, bureaucratic, and political.
‣ There was a chronic lack of commercial experience within the sponsorship group. In practical terms, this had the following consequences:

  - A hard negotiation stance upfront led to contractual terms that were unsustainable for the private contractor. The only way to make money as a consequence was to look for and then charge additional costs for changes in scope wherever possible.
  - Payment terms were unattractive. Ninety to one hundred days was standard. That followed an invoice approval process that often added further delay, as different departments sought to leverage the process for their benefit. This meant that public sector contracts were not viable for anyone but the very largest of private sector contractors who could manage their cashflow as a consequence of other work.

‣ A disconnect between the key performance indicators for the contractors (time and money) compared with the government sponsor, whose expectations were much broader and included legacy, environmental impact, and engagement of the community.

Ultimately, finding organizations that wanted to bid for this type of public sector work was becoming more and more difficult. When it came to identifying interested parties and inviting them to pitch for work at the London Olympics 2012, it was a major challenge to find anyone who was prepared to commit themselves. It is a little-known fact that, in the end, there was only one bidder for the construction of the main stadium.

A new way of contracting

One of the key changes to the above context was the introduction of an experienced layer of specialists from the building industry whose responsibility was to act as advisors and sit between government and the contractors tasked with the construction of the various venues.

Rather than depend on a few individuals to carry out this role, the approach was to contract directly with three well-known organizations to act in this intermediary capacity. This approach created a check and balance that had never existed before. It also enabled the engagement of some of the most senior and experienced people in the industry, in some cases the CEOs of the advisory group of companies.

This new approach encountered some early teething problems. Iteration became a core part of the learning process as government, contractors, and the advisory group started to respond to the different requirements. An early example was the alignment of key performance indicators (KPIs).

▸ In the initial contract between the ODA and the delivery partners, the KPIs were the standard ones used by government: time and budget. This was at odds with the ODA's own set of KPIs on which basis the bid had been successful. They included these two dimensions but also put a strong emphasis on the delivery of other factors. These included the environmental impact, quality, what was going to happen to the site post Olympics (described as legacy), and the long-term benefit for the local community. The site had been chosen specifically as a way of helping a relatively poor part of London to move forward in terms of employment, training, quality of infrastructure, etc.

▸ The alignment of these two divergent perspectives took place after a renegotiation halfway through the contracted period. It led to a more complex set of KPIs, but ones that were monitored closely by all stakeholders.

Finally, the new structure with its layer of expertise, deep relationships into the industry, and aligned set of performance indicators gave the overall organization a sense of confidence. Given the context of Wembley and the reputation of the UK government in delivering large infrastructure programs, this was really important. As one of my interviewees puts it, *'There was a sense that the organization knew its "shit." Our contractors felt that they could confidently be part of the structure and not lose money or put their reputation at risk by being involved in the program.'*

Leadership and a key set of principles

This perception of core competence came from the top. The concept of transparency, openness, courage, and trust is a core theme running through many of the stories in this book. David Higgins (CEO of LOCOG) exemplifies this in his behavior, communications approach, and approachability.

David had excellent credentials for the program. He came from the building sector as CEO at LendLease (the largest Australian building contractor) when the company was engaged to develop the Sydney Olympics 2000 site. His focus at LOCOG was on the legacy and on the impact on the site at Stratford. His approach mirrored best practice within program management. He recognized the interdependence between his implementation challenge and the supply chain early on, and looked for pragmatic ways to support them. *'We set out three years ago to pay within thirty days. We are now aiming for eighteen days. The best thing that we can do [for contractors] is to ensure early payment and run the site very competently.' (New Civil Engineer, January 6, 2009).*

One can see his influence in every aspect of the program. An example was the establishment of an early principle around health and safety even before any sites had been procured. London was the first Olympic Games in living memory where there were no fatalities. There was also clarity of expectation of his team with regard to risk. Not knowing the answer was acceptable; not reporting on an issue that represented risk was a sackable offense.

Communications

There is a refreshing similarity to the nature of successful communications in many of the successful transformation stories, and perhaps how simple in some ways these methods were.

▸ For the CEO, daily walkarounds became a core part of the communications process and a powerful way of gathering informal feedback and being accessible. Others in the leadership team followed his example.

▸ Every month, David would do a one-hour 'standup' to the entire ODA team. At the start, with a team of forty, this was comparatively easy to do, and for it to feel personal, but he maintained this process as the organization grew to two hundred, the levels of complexity and challenge developed similarly, and his own schedule became more and more challenging. Importantly, there was a sense that he was telling the organization the whole story: '...*when things got tough, he would explain this and perhaps comment on what was causing the issues. Everyone felt onboard and trusted him.*' These 'standups' became part of the core cadence within the ODA and set the tone for wider messaging as well.

A sense of purpose

Creating a sense of purpose became something very pragmatic and easily measurable. David's focus on tangible deliverables started in the first year of the program. He established a process where he would publish widely the ten things that would be achieved that year in January. Given the press scrutiny, the potential of being a hostage to fortune was enormous. For David, however, it represented a clarity of intent and purpose that was critical in managing and motivating the team. It also had the benefit of demonstrating confidence in the team's ability to deliver, which was really important for external stakeholders.

Thinking like an owner

This concept is at the heart of a lot of the successful transformation stories captured in this book. It relates to the idea that accountability is taken seriously at all levels of a program, enabling leadership to distribute decision making to the most appropriate level, rather than having to respond to indiscriminate escalation. For Ky Nichol, 'thinking like an owner' was at the core of successful implementation at the London Olympics.

Ky Nichol was part of the program management office for the Olympic Delivery Authority from 2005 to 2010, and helped to establish some early structures and core principles. He started his career in the space sector before a moving into program management. In 2017 he started a business called Cutover, an enterprise-wide change management platform, designed to enable collaboration at task level for large-scale, complex programs of change.

He gives an example in the London Olympics where the idea of ownership featured heavily. As mentioned earlier, the financial crisis put enormous pressure on certain aspects (the 'nice to haves') of the budget. Leadership was in no position to defend these requirements, and as a result funding for some of these projects had been cut dramatically.

For the LOCOG employees, cutting this aspect of the build was a compromise they were not prepared to accept. An initiative was started to develop a sponsorship / fundraising program to enable much of the original design plan to be completed. The fundraising was successful. As a result of this initiative, the most striking design feature was retained: the Anish Kapoor Orbit Tower, sponsored by Arcelor Mittal.

Governance 'fit for purpose'

There are a lot of references to governance in this book, often with regard to the inadequacy of existing 'business as usual' governance in the context of transformation. This relates particularly well to the need for fast decision making.

For the London Olympics, two themes emerge from the interviewees that are striking, not least in their simplicity.

The 80% rule

In a program of the scale of the Olympics, there are many stakeholders who have the power to say 'no' and in effect hold the program to ransom. While this might manifest itself as a stakeholder management challenge, the primary effect is on behavior. If there is a sense that this type of behavior is effective and leads to good results, the program as a whole will start to suffer.

The 80% rule is an agreement across all stakeholders that when they have reached 80% comfort with a particular decision, they will agree to move forward. The rule stems from a recognition that resolving the last 20% of any challenge is dispro-portionate. Most importantly, it can prevent progress and momentum across the program, which is fundamental for successful implementation.

Agreeing this in principle and implementing in reality are often two very different tasks. With senior LOCOG sponsorship and endorsement, the rule remained intact throughout the implementation phase, a testament to the alignment of stakehold-ers around this core program management principle.

Dashboards and reporting

The industry of program management has never been shy in the need and deploy-ment of large-scale resources to plan, review, update, and track progress. It is a regular criticism of large, complex programs that the process of tracking progress is often an industry in itself. The challenge, however, of getting the right information to the right people in a timely fashion is considerable.

One of the advantages for the program was the recruitment of a cohort of experi-enced leaders who had previously worked on major infrastructure programs. Using this knowledge, the team was able to rely on a dashboard process that gave a very quick overview of progress and hotspots for focus while minimizing the effort of developing this view.

The second challenge for reporting is transparency. Watermelon reporting (green on the outside, red under the skin) remains a challenge for most programs where reporting bad news is perceived to be detrimental to one's career prospects or consulting revenue going forward.

While it might appear that the solution to this problem is the establishment of a consistent framework for project managers around what constitutes the different statuses, that is only half the solution. The main challenge rests with early manage-ment of the leadership response to bad news. As ever, a single badly managed reac-tion to an issue that has been brought to leadership attention can set the program back by a number of months.

For the London Olympics, managing the messaging externally was a key first step in this process. From the start, leadership demonstrated real confidence and comfort with the normal risks and challenges of delivery to important external shareholders. This reinforced the willingness of those managing the component parts to be honest in their assessment of progress in the knowledge that this was being reflected accurately across the program.

Conclusion

It is perhaps easy to look at the Olympics and see very few learning points in our own transformation programs. Time scales, budgets, impact, all seem of such a vastly different scale that the relevance is hard to grasp.

Two things stand out, however, that are worth considering for any program going forward.

First, there is real value to the idea that each Olympic Games is effectively started from scratch. There was no playbook, and for good reason. The circumstances were very different from a budget, location, and political perspective. There was also an unwillingness on the part of previous incumbents to share their experiences, as well as a reluctance on the part of the new incumbent to ask questions. All of us have perhaps gone through that journey of discovery.

What is the value in that learning? It demonstrates that even for the most complex of programs, bringing a team together, engaging them in a common purpose, and giving them the space to operate are the secret ingredients.

The second thing worth considering is that the perceived risk of failure remains constant, no matter how large or small the program might be. In the case of the Olympics, it led to the need for very senior intervention (note the number of bidders willing to engage with LOCOG). It also led to the implementation of a set of simple principles that lasted and became part of the bedrock for success (the 80% rule).

For me, what stands out about this example is the lack of compromise in terms of ambition. The London Olympics remains the greenest Games ever delivered, and the success of its legacy is easy to see. What I will remember is how success stems from the deployment of small, easy to understand, practical, and pragmatic actions. Printing good quality updates, arranging bus tours, and maintaining standups as a primary method of communication over a seven-year period. None of those things were earth-shattering. They just added up to an incredible result.

GLH Hotels London: Building a unique identity in hospitality

Context

It is probably a little harsh to describe GLH Hotels as a vanity asset. The business had been bought and owned by a Malaysian conglomerate, Hong Leong, who were interested first and foremost in the property rather than the potential for a sensible return from their hotel business. The primary assets in this owner-operator group of hotels were London based. They were held under the brands of Thistle and Guoman. The Thistle Hotels chain had been characterized as the 'Little Chef' of British hotels, a ubiquitous, but unglamorous, functional brand. It was a brand that had previously proved entirely resistant to rebranding from its three-star status, which created a problem for the owners. The properties were in need of refurbishment, but the brand recognition was such that any attempt had the potential of imposing a four-star cost base on a three-star revenue stream.

The Guoman Hotels were a series of independently run hotels based in London. They were a legacy of an era where hotels were located close to railway stations. The sites were attractive in terms of location—Charing Cross, Marble Arch, and Victoria—but the original purpose and convenience had become irrelevant as the nature of travel changed.

The issue of scale

In the early 2000s, as booking moved online, the challenge of getting enough Internet traffic was an issue for a twenty-hotel chain in London. GLH's nearest comparison was the eight thousand hotels on the Wyndham site. Wyndhams themselves were being outmaneuvered and outspent (in terms of search engine optimization or SEO) by the eight hundred thousand hotels on the Expedia site or the million hotels on Booking.com, Google's biggest customer. The amount of money that was being spent buying Ad words by these groups was enormous. To consider the two and a half million rental properties on Airbnb was a further challenge of scale altogether.

For GLH Hotels, then, the challenge was to make a five-thousand-room owner-occupied hotel chain in central London relevant and distinctive in the age of Internet-based booking, large chains, and Airbnb. The starting position was not great. The hotels were very tired in terms of look and feel. Market perception was entrenched and not positive. The employee base was disengaged. Investment was required but resetting customer expectations on price was challenging.

A final bit of context: TripAdvisor was the new global currency, the primary method of measuring hotel customer value. TripAdvisor's rating was the primary driver in the process of getting customers and determining pricing. Consumers spent on average sixteen minutes on TripAdvisor prior to booking a hotel, and their main focus was guest experience reviews. GLH's TripAdvisor ratings were dire. Only 21% of the company's hotels were in the top quartile. This was reflected in the financial performance. Average profitability was at least 20% less than that of its competitors.

The path to transformation

Changing the leadership

Mike DeNoma was brought in as CEO with a specific focus on transformation. Mike's experience in transformation is extraordinarily wide and deep. He started his career in brand management with Proctor and Gamble before moving to PepsiCo, where he ran international operations across sixty-five countries. He moved to Singapore in 1989 with Citigroup. In 1999 he joined Standard Chartered Bank as Group CEO for the Global Consumer Bank and was appointed to the group board of directors in 2009. Mike spent a further three years in Taiwan as CEO for CTBC (a large local bank owned by private equity) and was responsible for the turnaround of the business. He became CEO of GLH in 2012 to manage the transformation program before returning to Asia in 2017 as CEO of KBZ Bank in Myanmar.

Another important hire for the transformation program was Alastair Campbell. Alastair started his career in strategy consulting before moving into the banking sector with Standard Chartered in Asia, where he was based for seven years. He had a series of senior strategy roles across of a range of sectors, including telco (Singtel), and hotels (GLH). He is currently Head of Group Strategy with RBS.

Alongside these two, a new CFO and CIO were also brought into the organization.

Bringing in a new management team is hardly a new idea when it comes to change. The real challenge is building some trust between that management team and the employee base. Mike describes the challenge as follows:

'If the employees think that your intention is "pure" and good for them, then they will follow. If not, forget it. People are cynical generally; they don't believe things are going to change. But if you ask them what their organization is about, they will give you the essence, not replay corporate affairs double-speak. My first job is to find out what the heartbeat of the organization is and to leverage that.'

Developing a sense of purpose

In my discussions with Mike and Alastair, it is interesting how this question generates a response that is less about the 'program' and more about identifying an inherent sense of purpose. This was not some 'behind closed doors' process but one that looked to engage the widest possible audience.

What did Mike find when he spoke to the employees at GLH?

'I found passion. They entered the industry to serve the guest. What I found in the hotel industry was the incredible human connection you can build with people when they come and stay with you. GLH did that incredibly well.

That's all fine. But the big challenge in the hotel industry is the socio-economic gap that exists between employees and their guests. In places like London, it's particularly large and it leads to a situation where the last thing any employee wants is to be asked a question. That's unlikely to end well...which is why you end up with all the blabberisms, all those meaningless phrases.'

Bridging the gap between the intent and the reality of working in a hotel became the main focus. Mike describes a series of roadshows:

'I got everyone to leave the room and when they came back, out of the 300 or so, 299 were given the role of a guest and one was a host. So then I would spend some time with this one person, the host. Ask him all sorts of questions. How do you act, what do you look like, are you a follower or a leader? etc. We were able to establish some really clear principles about what it was like to act the host.

> *The key point here was the word "act." Everyone knows what that's about. In every culture on earth, you act the host. You teach your kids, if their friends are over, their friends get it. If your next door neighbor who's a pain in the ass is over, it doesn't matter. He's your guest. Right? What do you do? You act the host.'*

He then captured the idea in a simple, four-word phrase for the organization.

> *'This is my house.'*

> *'If it's your house, you're going to act the host, and that's ok. You know instinctively what to do. That was really the genus of GLH.'*

Alastair Campbell describes the concept in a slightly different but equally compelling way:

> *'Hospitality and service are not the same thing. Service is the process of giving the customer what they want. If you want a cup of coffee, I'll run off and bring you a cup of coffee. Hospitality is the process of making you feel welcome. It's possible to get you a cup of coffee in an amazingly efficient and thoroughly responsive way. It is exactly what you needed, but somehow it doesn't leave you feeling welcome. It's also possible to get you a cup of coffee and mess it up a bit, spill a bit of coffee in the saucer, but to do so in a way that feels very warm and caring. Shock news. If you look on TripAdvisor, the second experience gets a much better response than the first.'*

Creating a virtuous feedback loop

An important early process was the development of a feedback process that was as close to real time as possible. Technology enablement was important in this process. One of the first steps in the refurbishment was to install top-of-the-range Wi-Fi across all hotels that would be free to use for guests and employees. Employees were equipped with iPads, which became the primary source of communications and work scheduling.

As part of this technology uplift, a feedback app was installed that provided instant feedback. This would vary from specific room-based issues to commentary on the overall experience of staying in the hotel. The feedback tool was open and visible to all.

As is often the case, the implementation of this tool was as important as the tool itself. Mike describes situations where he would see a piece of feedback from a guest very early in the morning (he usually rose around 0400). Examples included a shower not working, or a blown light bulb. He would pass the message on to the hotel GM immediately so that the issue could be swiftly resolved. This speed of response was established very quickly, and it created real urgency in the organization. It also demonstrated in a meaningful way that the leadership and the team were connected.

The second part was to share the positive feedback. Mike still remembers two comments that captured the incredible sense of purpose among the employee base.

The first was:

> 'I don't know what it is, but this hotel has an unbelievably positive vibe and feeling to it.'

The second was a specific comment with regard to the sense of caring in the organization:

> '...the other one that stays in my memory was this one where we had an older lady staying who suffered from arthritis. Every morning the maid would help her put on her socks.'

Mike comments that hotel employees were not generally used to getting feedback. The impact then of immediate positive reinforcement for their individual and collective actions was extraordinary. It became a driving force for the organization, and generated amazing energy. Alastair describes the process as follows:

> 'The thing that really made it special was that we set an outrageous goal of totally self-generated performance. The target for every hotel was to try and achieve ninety "radical hosting" moments every day. Every employee had, with their iPad or their phone, the ability to record any radical hosting moments

that they achieved, anything they did with "caring and kindness." The instructions were simple: "Send it in and we're going to record it, celebrate success, and validate the process."'

What sort of things were typically recorded?

'Little things like someone noticing a long queue at the concierge and opening another desk to help some more people through. An electrician being made aware that the light in a bathroom on 2019 was off and coming down from the seventh floor, where his rota had him working, and fixing it within two minutes of the call from the customer.

The whole thing was clearly open for corruption; you could make it all up, but the point was, we are just ourselves. We are us, you know, there's nothing else. We are trying to create London's friendliest, warmest hotel chain. And that means that even if you think your job is to be a concierge, or to be an electrician, or to be a cleaner, actually your job is to make the people here feel welcome.'

What's particularly powerful about this answer is that it combines honesty with identity. Thinking back to the Nextel case study, there are some strong similarities.

How did these little moments translate into improved performance?

'The micro effects are more important that the macro ones. If a customer noted in his feedback form that the shower in room 301 wasn't very good, that feedback came directly through to the engineers, who saw it as their responsibility to fix it immediately, not to wait until 301 came up as part of the rota. If we noted that customer satisfaction scores for 405 were consistently worse than for other rooms on that floor, we would refurbish that room straightaway, not wait until the fourth floor in general was due for refurbishment.'

Performance measurement

Taking decentralization and autonomy to a new level

The role of General Managers in hotels has steadily been diminished with the advent of group functions who control everything from housekeeping, front of house, food and beverage, to operations and maintenance. While the purpose is understandable in the search for operational efficiency, it has steadily shifted decision making from those closest to the customer to remote leadership, which has very little contact with the guest. As Alastair put it:

> *'Hotel managers are managers in name only in the hospitality industry. They are operational people; they don't actually run anything. It's not in the interest of a franchise to have someone local managing the hotel.'*

For GLH, the owner-operator nature of the group was critical in enabling a major shift in decision making to take place.

The change was encapsulated in the concept of Value Centers, which were established in each hotel. These value centers were accountable for linking sales and revenue management with operational cost centers and resource management, giving them end-to-end accountability for value creation, including profitability. Strategy was developed at value center level, with the development of performance targets.

The role of the functions and the value centers shifted dramatically. In the past, decisions were made in the center and imposed on the hotels. As a consequence of the change in accountability, value center teams were now in a position to pull support from head office and other areas to meet their strategic and operational needs.

The real power of this change becomes clear when looking at some examples. Alastair talks about the revenue generation aspect:

> *'If you want to drum up business among corporates in your location, the best way is to pitch to corporates who have businesses that are located around your hotel. It's stunningly obvious. And the best way to pitch to them is to have the GM of the hotel go around to them and find out what they need. If there's*

a problem, "I'm the GM. You have my number and I'm literally next door." As opposed to ringing some central help desk!'

It is worth looking at a specific example to see how this process of decentralization actually worked.

The Tower Hotel

The Tower Hotel, situated just north of Tower Bridge on the edge of the City of London, was one of the largest in the group, with eight hundred rooms in total. For one GM, selling eight hundred rooms for three hundred and sixty-five days is an enormously challenging target. The start of every year therefore was to do a lot of 'base' business. This involved going to tour operators for low cost, block bookings.

By splitting the hotel into four value centers, each value-center GM now had two hundred rooms to sell. This reduced the pressure to build a book early. As the results show, the impact on pricing and profitability was dramatic.

Selling strategies also started to reflect the value center. For those GMs with a portfolio of basic rooms, campaigns that emphasized the convenience and discounted the rooms appropriately improved occupancy and customer experience. GLH pioneered the concept of a 'crash pad,' which you could stay in if you had a late event in the city at a deeply discounted rate.

Mike makes the point that this decentralization process was valuable from two perspectives: First, the connection to customer need became paramount. Second, those who had the responsibility were trained and mentored to deliver it. Having been given responsibility to think about strategy, they were expected to communicate their plans clearly, talk coherently about them with their colleagues and the leadership group, implement the plans, and manage the process. He says:

'We created a whole new generation of General Managers who were the best in the business. They really knew their stuff. They became hugely employable across the industry.'

Innovation aligned to purpose

The challenge of competing with much larger groups created the need to innovate. Finding opportunities to differentiate GLH from the competition became an ongoing challenge. One of the more successful ideas was the 'Choose your room' initiative.

In contrast to Airbnb, the decision to choose a hotel room is based on a false premise. The photographs of the former are invariably of the actual apartment or room that you're going to stay in. That is very rarely the case for the photos that are used to advertise rooms in a hotel.

For the vast majority of hotel guests, that is not significant. There are, however, distinct groups for whom the floor, the location of the room on the floor, and / or the need to have adjoining rooms are important decision-making criteria. Those of you who have tried to book family rooms only to be forced into an uncomfortable compromise will recognize the challenge.

The 'Choose your room' initiative was designed to cater for guests who had these specific needs. Because GLH was entirely integrated, the Web site gave access to all fifteen hotels and enabled guests to make an informed choice based on their specific needs.

The facility was available only to those booking directly through the GLH Web site. It therefore drove up Web site traffic and direct bookings. The latter was also extremely valuable from a profitability perspective, as no intermediary payments were required. For Booking.com, this amounts to a staggering 30% of room cost.

Results

Above and beyond the financial and ratings improvement, which are set out below, the GLH story is a remarkable one. Perhaps uniquely it charts a transformation journey that combines the opportunity for individuals to bring their own personalities to the workplace with the power of the collective. It demonstrates the power of autonomy at every level. 'Real-time' feedback creates an immediate set of priorities for all, irrespective of rank or position. It also enables those making decisions to use their intuition. Purpose becomes the performance drug for the organization. Leadership and employees are totally connected, and bound by the same psychological contract.

Conclusion

How did GLH Hotels do? The results are remarkable. For the three years prior to transformation, the business was ranked approximately seventy-fifth in terms of profitability in its sector and grouping. According to TripAdvisor, its customer satisfaction ratings put GLH firmly in the fourth quartile, with only two hotels in the top quartile.

During transformation, all of the key performance indicators (guest satisfaction, employee engagement, and profitability) have improved simultaneously. Average profitability across the group has gone up to more than 14%, double that of its competitors with an EBITDA per room of over 80%.

Its Trip Advisor ratings also changed dramatically with thirteen of the fifteen hotels ranking in the top quartile and more than 25% of the rooms being in the top 10%. This was achieved while maintaining labor costs, increasing occupancy levels, and increasing room rates in line with its competitors over the period. The progression for individual hotels was particularly remarkable. The AMBA (following rebranding, the chain was renamed AMBA) Charing Cross went from being two hundred and twentieth in 2013 to sixth in 2016.

03
A FRAMEWORK

A framework based on experience, not theory

The second half of this book gives a perspective on the prerequisites for being successful at transformation. The format for giving you this insight is very similar to that of the first half of this book. It is in the context of a set of stories from my interviews. The stories have large sections that are virtually verbatim from my interviews. For me, this is key. The language that they use, the messy nature of their discovery process, the emotional highs and lows, this is the place where learning and transformation really take place. What I have set out is a framework that you can adhere to or indeed learn from.

...not a model

A framework is not a model. To define them both, frameworks have some principles based on experience, some useful hints, and a direction of travel that is broad enough to accommodate divergence and difference. In other words, they are not prescriptive.

Models are detailed descriptions of best practice with artefacts, fact sheets, and frequently asked questions and checklists to help with navigation. The stage gate is a frequent feature with a handy checklist as to what needs to be provided, in what format, and who the audience should be. The Excel spreadsheets that form part of the artefacts are pre-programed and linked so that anyone picking one up off the shelf has to spend a couple of days learning how to navigate their way around them. The model often also comes with a handily preprepared set of PowerPoint slides as guidance for what 'good' reporting looks like.

All of this looks great when you're concluding a program of work with the client. It captures the artefacts that you've worked through. The client and you share some memories of the time when the status report had to be changed to accommodate a stakeholder's particular whim about font size or style, or the fact that it couldn't be easily printed on one page without being impossible to read. It reminds you both of the journey.

Your journey is not, however, the same as my journey. I don't care why you decided to go for Times New Roman as opposed to Arial. My client likes color, but not that awful pink hue which seems to be all-pervasive in your Risk Register (is it red or something less than red in terms of issue). Neither of us understands why there isn't an automatic numbering system in the program plan template. I don't understand why, when I try to put one in, it messes all of the other linked columns up so that the dashboard is now gobbledygook!

Most of all, I'm annoyed because my client and I had some really interesting ideas on how to manage this process, measure progress, and keep reporting to a minimum. Those ideas have been sabotaged by your framework, which was supposedly 'so easy' to follow. My focus has moved from encouraging the right types of behavior among the team to completing the framework.

The impact is real. In a recent transaction, I worked with a very large financial services business with a Resource Management Model that was core to their resource allocation for transformation work. The model had obviously been designed to encourage transparency of work, collaboration across functions to ensure that SMEs were being used most effectively, and as a way of providing some data on the cost of implementation. Sadly, what it actually did was to actively encourage employees to charge hours for work they had not done, based on zero assessment of quality and no control. There were no limits to how long retrospectively this process was allowed to happen. In the particular case I was dealing with, that amounted to over £1.3 million of accruals from between eleven and seven months ago.

To summarize the framework

In the following sections, I identify, through the stories, three different conditions for transformation. Those conditions are Process, Purpose, and Plasticity. The last is a condition on its own, but also a consequence of the other two.

I also look at different ecosystems as the basis for encouraging or discouraging these conditions to occur.

As a first step in considering this framework, it is valuable to think about how transformation has worked in your organization in the past. Which condition did you find most effective, and what were the short – and long-term results? It is also useful to have a look at the ecosystems described and see if you recognize any of the features in your own business.

Introduction

The PPP framework has three components, Process, Purpose, and Plasticity. In addition, there are two other concepts that are important in the framework: the idea of a corporate ecosystem, and the role of momentum in transformation.

Process: Process is an inheritance from the industrial revolution. In the context of a company, its primary role is to standardize ways of working and ultimately reduce risk around quality, performance, and delivery. Process represents the flip side of purpose...it says, 'Follow me,' and everything else will take care of itself.

From a human perspective it has other benefits. It removes stress and enables our mental capacity to focus on meaningful, creative, intellectually taxing, left-brained requirements. It plays to our tendency to commit to ways and methods of working, based on positive outcomes. Good processes are born out of experience, and retrospectively re-engineered to great effect.

Every organization has core processes deeply embedded in the culture and ways of working. Many organizations have non-core processes that are no longer fit for purpose, create additional complexity, and add little value.

Purpose: Purpose is the greatest driver of change that we possess. Purpose also defines our daily existence, from the most basic requirements of security and nourishment, to the more esoteric and equally necessary requirements of meaning and contribution. A shared purpose creates a bond between employees and their employer. Organizations that have a sense of purpose appear to defy gravity and time in terms of expectations around implementation. Employees who are driven by a sense of purpose find meaning in the most menial of tasks.

Purpose is **not** strategy! Strategy is driven by rational thinking. Purpose in organizations touches employees at a much deeper, emotional level, connects with their personal values, and creates an intrinsic willingness to collaborate. Purposeful organizations do not spend the first quarter of any meeting providing context for decisions, direction, and plans...these things are intrinsically understood. Purposeful organizations iterate seamlessly between direction and execution. They change direction because their purpose drives them there.

Plasticity: The concept of plasticity spans biology, psychology, and physics, and its definition does not vary greatly across those disciplines. It signifies the capacity to be molded or altered.

In the context of a transformation program, the concept of plasticity is useful. It suggests an adaptive quality, but not without some structure or rigidity. This is not difficult to understand. Everyone knows and can instantly recognize both texturally and at a conceptual level the difference between jelly and Play-doh. It is part of most people's childhood experience to have at some stage played with and perhaps marveled at the qualities of both.

Plasticity is the critical precondition necessary for any transformation. It can be defined as a unique combination of elasticity, flexibility, and the infinite opportunity for iteration with the right amount of energy.

The concept of iteration is perhaps the most important component of plasticity, and has a key role to play in transformation. Iteration is how we as children learn. It is therefore something we instinctively turn to, when given license to do so. It has no barriers in terms of human capability; it stretches across all aspects of human experience from artists to engineers to those who deliver major programs of work.

Ecosystem: I have co-opted the concept of a corporate ecosystem to describe a complex, all-encompassing view of an organization. To use a metaphor, it includes an organization's component parts or its chemistry (people, machinery, systems) and its integrators or physics (culture, core processes, networks and relationships, leadership, teams, and informal structures).

The key word in the above description is 'complexity.' Complexity in the above context is not down to laziness or a lack of curiosity and intellect to develop something simple. Complexity is core in any business because it reflects its main component...us. Throughout this book you will read descriptions of organizations, some of which you may know. They will probably contradict your own conclusions. It is highly likely that we are both right. This is part of the human experience of working within a business where even those sitting right next to each other may have a subtly or dramatically different experience.

In this book, you are going to read about good and bad ecosystems, and probably many that sit in between. Bad ecosystems are ones where the conditions positively discriminate against successful transformation programs.

Momentum: A final component for consideration as part of the framework for successful transformation. In delivering transformation programs, pace and time are regularly the only measure of success. This is not because there are no quality expectations and no budget; it merely reflects the fact that these are rarely clear and unambiguous. Defining success based on time alone appears so simple.

The 'delivery' reality of time is fundamentally different. Does an Enterprise Resource Planning implementation (ERP) end when the new system is in place, or when it's been fully adopted and the shadow systems have been turned off? Is a post-deal integration program complete at the end of a Transition Services Agreement (TSA), or when there is a single set of products and services for the customer? Both answers are potentially correct but represent a very different understanding of completion from the perspective of time.

The PPP Framework identifies three different drivers and methods for transformation. Each driver has a different dynamic and outcome.

- -

What to do with the PPP framework
The framework provides an opportunity for a bit of well-structured, indulgent introspection. I would encourage you to ask yourself, and perhaps those around you, some questions:

- *What are the key dimensions of my organization's ecosystem (chemistry and physics)? Are they helpful or not helpful in terms of transformation?*
- *How have they affected previous attempts to transform, innovate, change, or integrate?*
- *Is there an intuitive, emotionally engaging, and easily explained sense of purpose in our business, one that you could explain to someone from outside the company? What is the evidence, anecdotal or otherwise, that what we do touches our employees in a meaningful way?*
- *Does our business have process management embedded within it? Is the motivation to follow those processes based on 'carrot' or 'stick'?*

The answers to these questions will begin to reveal what is possible in your organization, and what constraints exist.

Beyond the diagnostic phase, the next phase is to identify some key internal challenges to which your organization is going to have to respond in the short and medium term. These could be the capacity at leadership level, the appetite for risk, etc.

If you can start to set out the barriers and enablers to successful implementation, you will have a fair chance of succeeding.

A final point. Program leadership, M&A integration, the CEO role...the insight of my interviewees seems to suggest that all these three things are *'different sides of the same coin,'* to quote my good friend and colleague, David Boyd. All three drive change, often through a sense of purpose (which is not always there when you start), build a team that functions well and trusts each of the component parts, tracks progress (qualitative and quantitative), learns through iteration and making mistakes, celebrates the smallest and largest success, and rewards the right behaviors.

A CEO is in place for a period of time to drive change. Program management doesn't just have 'things' in common with being a CEO...it is everything for a CEO and vice versa.

Process: Managing risk is all that matters

Humans have a love / hate relationship with process. On one hand, it sits completely at odds with our sense of our individuality, which is at the core of our identity. On the other hand, we are remarkably resistant to anything that might upset the core processes in our lives. I often ask a new group of program and change managers a couple of specific questions at the start of any new engagement.

'Did you take a different route to get to work this morning?'

'Your coffee today—did you get it in a different place from usual?'

These are banal questions. They are not material in the context of one's life. You would think that they would not provide any stress at all, just a bit of variety. Yet even for this group of professional people who are probably exposed to change more than most and make a living out of corporate change, the answers are almost invariably 'No.' The reason is obvious and scientifically proven. Change leads to stress, and stress is life-shortening.

Our love affair with process stems from our attraction to collective behavior. We are gregarious animals. Benedict Anderson, in his book *Imagined Communities* (1983), famously writes about this idea in the context of a nation coming together in its actions, whether that's in reading newspapers, watching the nine o'clock news, or, in a peculiarly British way, sitting down after our Christmas lunch to listen to the Queen's speech.

We find comfort in the boundaries of our decision-making ability as set by others in leadership or positions of influence. We find comfort in the sense of belonging arising from a collective intent and set of activities.

Beyond the collective intent, where does our willingness to adhere to process come from? It turns out that there are a number of drivers:

▸ The first is where the alternative represents physical danger. Health and Safety is the clear non-negotiable that provides impetus, not only for ourselves, but perhaps more importantly and more usefully in the context of a transformation program, for our friends and colleagues. The motivation to follow a process so as not to endanger those around us is very strong. In sectors where that threat is constant (Oil and Gas, Primary, Heavy Industry), the opportunity to leverage this motivation into a corporate culture that adheres to process is both logical and relatively easy to implement. The experience of 2020-21 with Covid 19 reflects this willingness to conform in the presence of danger to others.

▸ The second driver is one where there is a meaningful threat of personal and corporate sanction from a regulatory, governmental body. There is nothing like the imminent prospect of imprisonment or being fined extraordinary amounts of money to create the sort of single-minded focus that leads to process harmonization at the micro level. One of the interviewees when describing the culture of her organization provided an interesting insight into her regional CEO which illustrates this perfectly. *'He spreadsheets his day, he micro-manages every minute.'* The effort to achieve this is enormous in terms of documentation, reinforcement of the rationale, and the behavioral change required. It is because of this significant effort that it becomes the dominant characteristic of the business.

▸ Process conformity also becomes a driver where the potential for reputational risk extends from impacting a corporation to directly affecting individuals. A good example is the world of Non-Executive Directorships (NED) in the UK. The risk profile for an NED has changed as the concept of personal liability has become more acute. Where once they were a reward for previous effort with little pressure and a small stipend as payment, the expectations of attendance and engagement these days are taken much more seriously.

Let's look at these three drivers in turn to see how they create change in a transformation program.

Physical danger

One of my interviewees worked at a global Oil and Gas company during a major separation and integration process in Southeast Asia. In this company, the rules and resultant processes around Health and Safety were stringent and rigorously enforced. A few examples from my conversation with him:

'The first meeting I attended in an older, not particularly well looked after, office building in Kuala Lumpur started in an unusual way. The Chair of the meeting (the role had been allocated earlier and was part of the invitation)

*started the meeting with an extensive Health and Safety briefing (the exits are here and here, don't use the lifts, the assembly point is here, the messaging system through the loudspeaker system will sound like this, keep calm, etc.). My initial response was, 'That's thoughtful, they are doing this for my benefit, perhaps for any newcomer to the office, very sensible.' It was only after the fourth meeting with a similar crew after I'd been there for a few days when the exact same thing happened that I finally understood...this happens at **every** internal meeting.*

When I was leaving the building, the receptionist very kindly wished me a good afternoon and exhorted me to use the handrail down the stairs to the front door.

On getting into a taxi with some colleagues from the business, it was made clear to me that everyone had to put on their seatbelt prior to the taxi moving off...this was more of a direct instruction rather than a polite request.

On a couple of occasions, employees were publicly ticked off for not wearing shoes walking around the office floor and in particular stepping into the kitchen in this "partially clad" manner where the possibility for pouring boiling water on to oneself existed.

Directly opposite the building was a local food court where the majority of employees ate lunch. To access this building, there were two routes. The first was to cross a small road (access only to the company) and one other building with limited traffic and one lane, the second was to turn right, walk for around 50 meters, use the zebra crossing, and return on the other side. It was deemed a sackable offence to take the direct route.'

It is easy to mock these examples and challenge the basis on which they are enforced. What is more interesting, however, is the all-pervading nature of this type of adherence culture. From a conformity perspective, the business has been incredibly successful in inculcating the principles of health and safety to every possible level and action within the business.

Melissa Almasi is head of transaction and delivery for a private equity global education / school business with a program management background in large transactions from her days with the Big Four. She gives a great example of this conformity to process in action. Her example has an industry-wide 'health and safety' perspective.

'My client was a major multinational utilities energy provider going through a major separation process [the sale of a division or business unit]. The business they were looking to sell was strong and well regarded but represented a part of the sector that was no longer core to their business. They had a highly intelligent, very efficient workforce. It was a big business, but size didn't seem to be detrimental to efficiency. All the people knew exactly what they were doing.

They had incredibly well-defined processes and instructions of how to do things. That was a legacy of one of their CEOs who had managed to implement that sense of uniformity across the entire business, from some of their operating assets sites all the way up to HQ. There was a simple expectation that you had to follow the process, no choice. It was the global construct. Risk aversion sat the heart of everything they did.'

There's a really interesting part of our interview when she starts to talk about the communication surrounding the separation. She describes the extraordinary sensitivity to information being given or leaked to the market, which might then need to be changed:

'We risked coming out with a perceived "half-truth" around transformation and then a few weeks later actually announcing that we're going to do a major divestiture. From our perspective, the risk that that would create was too large to take on. It was not worth it. The main priority of this whole deal, because of the assets that they had, was to maintain health and safety, "no fatalities on site." They knew from past experience that with any distraction there was the potential for employees to take their eye off the ball and that might cost people's lives.'

The same conformity to process based on risk / health and safety can also be a factor in an acquisition. In the next example, the transformation program was the large acquisition of a Southeast Asian food manufacturer by a well-known multinational. The challenge described here is as much about health and safety as it is about corporate reputation. The interviewee, a program director with responsibility for supporting the due diligence process and ultimately managing the integration program, describes the situation:

'During a site visit of one of the manufacturing plants in the north of the country, as part of the operational due diligence process, one of the visitors from the US noticed that most of the employees were wearing flip-flops while on the production line. He casually mentioned this as an issue to address at a meeting a few weeks later in the US, where one of the attendees was the Global Head of Health and Safety...who turned a little paler than normal.

Soon after, the missive came out that all new employees would be given a pair of safety boots on day one as part of their induction process. We had to point out to him that the process of introducing these did not start and end with the issuance of boots...but rather with an informal (through the existing hierarchies) communication process where the core value of taking responsibility for the health and safety of all employees was one of the key drivers of management. This was followed by the provision of lockers for all employees where they could change their footwear on starting and completing their shift. Most importantly from a cultural perspective, we also needed to give a firm date at which time the transition needed to be completed after which there would be no tolerance for non-conformity.

I should say, the previous leadership was not in any way "uncaring" of their employees...you just need to look at retention levels to see that. No, it was just a different set of priorities.'

Fear of sanction

Let us now look at the second driver: regulatory sanction. While it could appear that this might only be relevant in certain industries (financial services, pharmaceuticals) where specific governmental regulators exist to provide guidance and sanction for the good of the consumer, we live in an era of increased regulation. Any attempt to buy a listed business is also subject to regulatory scrutiny. Governmental influence over accounting standards acts as an all-encompassing, if indirect, method to regulate business activity. Climate change requirements have an impact on production standards and waste. The latter is important, not just because of the threat of sanction, but also because of the impact on employee sentiment.

Richard Cooper is a COO of long standing within the insurance industry, and has been based in Asia for more than ten years. His experience includes European as well as Asian businesses. His background and focus over his career has been large transformation programs, mostly in the context of M&A.

In his example of a major internal merger within a very large European insurance company, he focuses a great deal on the concept of clarity: clarity of purpose, clarity of operating model, clarity of systems requirements, clarity of ways of working, etc. This is captured in process documentation, role descriptions, and workflow structures. In his example, process sits at the heart of the integration. Part of this is also clarity of 'scope,' which is something I will explore later, a key dimension in process-led transformation.

Need for nuance

Adherence to process is not necessarily as simple as it sounds. There are some conditions that need to be met in order to have success using process as the transformation method of choice.

The employee base is an important consideration

What also comes out of my interview with Richard Cooper is the basis on which employees are prepared to commit themselves to a process-led transformation. He describes this as *'an instinctive and deep-seated loyalty and trust between employee and employer.'*

The acceptance of change through a highly structured, process-led approach (which in this case is part of the corporate and actually national culture for the business) is only possible when it is underpinned by an expectation and belief that whatever happens to the individual, they will be treated well. This, by the way, applies not just to those who may be directly affected by the planned change (those being made redundant) but also those around them. The perception of fairness is critical here.

It is clear, then, that process works as a method for transformation where process conformity is generally accepted and forms part of the DNA of the business impacted. In the example of the Southeast Asian food manufacturing acquisition mentioned above, the employee base has a high and ultimately influenceable base of engineers. In this cohort, the concept of adherence to process is entirely logical and perceived to be the 'only' way to deliver anything.

This adherence to process can also extend beyond the employee base and into the external consulting / advisory community. In my interview with Melissa Almasi, she suggested that this expectation was in two parts: first, that consultants, lawyers, accountants, and any other non-core service support individually and collectively demonstrated a similar approach to dealing with transformation; second. that their knowledge of processes that were specific to the organization was extensive and part of their qualification for working there.

Conformity is not blind!

In process-oriented organizations, challenge becomes a powerful tool, if only because of its sparing usage. One of my interviewees describes a situation where a senior engineer was engaged to challenge timelines and scope of the overall plan based on his previous knowledge. She explains the impact of that:

> 'They brought in one of those people with a brilliant mind but also someone who everyone trusted. He questioned everything, in particular structure. We ended up replicating the structure of the new organization in the implementation process. That was brilliant, because all those new leaders had the opportunity to get their heads around their specific area of responsibility while the organization was still evolving. They ended up presenting their structure and role definitions to the ExCo. That kind of business leadership was invaluable... it was both ownership and definition at a time when the business was at its most pliable and it became part of the culture to have that kind of iterative discussion and debate. It was their time to collectively define what they were going to be going forward.'

Beyond the culture change, what this example provides is a fascinating insight into an organization where challenging the status quo is possible only for certain individuals (those with credibility and with the explicit agreement of leadership). However, what starts as something that an individual is allowed to do is rapidly then adopted as a modus operandi for the future.

How to deliver a process-led transformation irrespective of sector or threat of sanction

What happens in sectors where the threat to life is less obvious and where the prospect of financial sanction is unlikely? Is it still possible to use a similar approach, and, if so, are there any levers beyond sanction and reward? What are the implications of this approach in terms of other aspects of employee capability and performance? Ultimately, does the cost benefit analysis stack up?

There is a series of other levers that leadership can pull to enable process-based transformation to be effective.

The 'conform or leave' lever

For many of you, this will be familiar. From my experience, it seems to be most often applied in extreme remedial situations where the immediate strategic choice is at its most stark. One sees some aspects of it in the Nextel case study.

Stephen Helberg is a senior Risk Management professional who has operated in many different parts of the world and in different industries, from Financial Services to Oil and Gas and the Primary Industries.

He describes a scenario in one of his stories that captures the 'conform or leave' driver perfectly.

> 'In the early 2000s, a leading Australian multinational was criticized severely by the media and the investment advisory community for the fact that it did not appear to have a strategy. Beyond that, its ability to actually execute projects successfully was questionable. At that time, the annual project management was upwards of $800 million. Its price-earning ratio was lower than the other organizations in the sector because of this lack of visibility, communication, strategy and execution capability.
>
> The then CEO identified the issue as being the organization's ability to translate business strategy in tangible, tactical plans, specifically in the middle tier of a thirteen-level organization structure between CEO and new employee. His first step was to collapse the organization into seven levels. As part of that process, he required the organization to be assessed to see whether they could actu-

ally do that transition. Lots of people left as a consequence. There were clear guidelines. "If you're working at level five, this is the cognitive ability you need to operate across multi multiple jurisdictions, multiple operations and think organizationally. If you don't have that, it is going to be almost impossible for you to take a strategy and translate that into a set of tactical implementation plans and change the organization."'

It is worth noting some of the language the organization uses:

'What are the mechanisms that you can put in place to increase your confidence in our ability, the capability, capacity to execute?'

The story of the organization and the transformation program they went through was written up subsequently as a case study by a UK-based academic. One comment in particular is interesting, providing some context to the process of transformation being deployed:

'Many great strategic plans will not get from execution to delivery because the execution plan does not manage risk effectively.'

It is an example of where business process and organizational structure were used to create an environment that required absolute, total conformity to strategic direction. The approach was anchored in the concept of organizational risk with minimal tolerance for variation. There was no option here to challenge, question, provide feedback, or comment. All iteration was deemed unnecessary and a distraction from the purpose, which was clear and well articulated. The organization became an execution machine that followed instructions and delivered to a plan.

The 'manage your scope to death, ignore everything else' driver

Any program manager knows that managing scope is a critical exercise in any transformation program. In a process-oriented transformation program, understanding the organizational structure is also important. It enables the program manager to know who the stakeholders are and what position they occupy. It also gives a 'business as usual' picture of existing accountability. It is worth taking a step back to explain this phenomenon.

- Process-led transformation requires a clearly articulated and enforced functional structure within which to operate. This is necessary to limit the intervention to the specific part or process of the business that is being transformed.
- Functional stakeholders accept accountability, and are fiercely protective of their part of the organizational structure. That includes activity as well as people. However, they are equally fierce about things that do not fall within this space. Managing scope is in their interest.
- The possibility of failure and blame is a much greater risk than the potential benefit of exceeding a particular target. This is a corporate version of the 'loss aversion' bias, a concept in behavioral economics that suggests that humans feel loss much more keenly than they enjoy gain. Opportunities for ancillary benefits are therefore ignored.

This, by the way, is not a passive, 'we'll get to this later' decision taken in the hope that it goes away. It is an active decision, to paraphrase, 'that does not fall within the scope of my responsibility, I'm therefore opposed to it, and the potential benefits are meaningless as I will not be measured on them.'

One of my interviewees is a senior program director with over twenty years' experience working on large transformation programs within the UK banking sector. Most of his work has come from a technology challenge or, in this case, a major regulatory change. In this story he talks about a major omission in the scope of work that would have had serious consequences had it not been picked up by one of his program managers.

He describes the reaction of his MD below:

'My Accountable Executive was the MD for a very large part of the business, reporting to the board. When I told him of the challenge [some additional scope that was critical for the success of the program but that had only been identified twelve months into implementation], he was really unhappy. Not with the required scope change; he recognized that. It was just the additional risk that he was going to have to commit to. He had confidence that we would deliver the scope we had, but anything incremental made him really uncomfortable. In his mind, we were getting far too close to the delivery timeline. This was despite the fact that we still had eight, ten months to go.'

This fear of failure and blame extends to opportunities that would seem to be beneficial, with minimal additional cost or risk of delivery. The example below is a case in point:

> 'As a result of the work we'd done, we found two incredible opportunities for process improvement; they literally just fell into our lap.
>
> The first one related to customer onboarding. As a result of our work, we had basically process-mapped the entire bank end-to-end processes and found lots of holes, duplicate information, data coming from all over the place. The onboarding process was just a mess. So I went and had a chat with the COO for the commercial bank, and I told him, "We're looking at this, we reckon we could reduce onboarding time for new customers by 35% just by removing duplication, let alone any kind of process improvement." But they just weren't interested.
>
> The second one was around documentation for products, client forms, AML, KYC, etc. As part of our overall program, we had catalogued the entire commercial bank's documentation, which they'd never done before. You can imagine, this stuff just grows incrementally. We asked them whether, while we were doing this, they wanted us to put in a configuration control process, but, again, they were not interested.'

Managing employees in a process-led transformation

While process-led transformation does not put the employee base at the heart of the program, it does recognize their existence and, probably more importantly, their ability, conscious or otherwise, to influence the outcome. Even in highly regulated environments that lean toward a very structured, process-oriented approach, there is room for human capital-based intervention.

In an extraordinary success story that I referenced above, John Monk talks about the sale of an Ecuadorian bank subsidiary of Lloyds Bank. This was part of a strategy post financial crisis that resulted in a wholesale restructure and sale of the international elements of the bank. Selling banks has a peculiar dynamic that is perhaps common to service businesses where the ability to retain customers during the program is critical to maximizing value. Retaining customers while making the employee base redundant is a particularly difficult juggling act.

In this case, the introduction of people-oriented processes (workshops to support employees in their interview technique and CV writing) was a significant factor in customer retention. This is how he describes the process:

> 'Staff activities became a major focus, both financially and in terms of my personal attention. Those activities were a series of workshops and individual sessions for every single member of staff to teach them two things. One, how to write a CV, and two, how to interview for a job. Remember, most of them had been with us for a long time, these were new skills, and the prospect of being without work was frightening. They went through classroom activities offsite. They took time out of work. We put HR resources and all of the Executive Committee team into hitting their contacts with all of the other banks and other companies and other industries to find jobs for them.
>
> Everyone, from the most junior admin staff who'd only been there a couple of years to the senior managers, came out of that process and felt that the organization was looking after them.'

The results were remarkable: 95% of the business of the bank was successfully transferred away. They successfully placed all the staff and shut down the two branches. John comments:

> 'We were 20% better than the target for the full transfer. There was a net increase in the sale value based upon the transfer of value at close, which meant that the buyer had to find more funds! That was a remarkable result.
>
> For me, though, the effort put in and the outcome [the number of those who did not find another role to move to was in single digits] actually de-stressed the entire process and made the project team a part of the wider family of the business, enhancing the efforts of the staff during the process.'

A final comment on the process-driven nature of the transformation. Within Lloyds, there was a recognized process for divestiture, a play book that had been deployed previously, and an expectation from senior leadership that this was the approach that would be taken, and to a large extent it was. The success of the program did not come from a radical reshaping of this approach, but from the addition of certain small steps that responded directly to the needs of the employee base.

What's not possible with process-driven transformation?

The role of the external challenger...is changing possible without an external intervention?

There is a common theme in all the stories above. Success is at least partially due to an external force, either in the form of a respected individual who challenges the status quo, or because the situation is so dire that other ways of working need to be considered. The adherence to process and structure, job descriptions and reporting lines creates so much internal friction that change becomes extremely difficult to sustain.

Speed of implementation

The second major downside of process-led implementation is speed. Process-led transformation depends on an orderly, highly structured approach to business case, gathering of scope and requirements, resource identification and allocation, and introduction of new governance. This type of set-up lends legitimacy to the program. It enables stakeholders to commit without fear of personal risk. It creates momentum. The cost, however, is time, precisely at a moment in any program where time is precious. The point about anticipation is important. We unconsciously start to adapt to a new environment to protect ourselves from the uncertain.

The window where change is anticipated after an acquisition is six months. If nothing happens in that time frame, the expectation from an employee is that the status quo returns.

Elina Niemela has spent her career moving between complex program leadership roles and line management. She has had more than fifteen years' experience working in international and domestic integration programs for a number of large Finnish industrial conglomerates. Elina comes from an HR practice background and brings her experience in dealing with people and change to bear.

In our discussion she described a recent business experience in which, despite apparent attempts to integrate, employees still associated themselves closely with the previous employer and brand. In a number of cases, this was almost ten years after the acquisition was completed. The impact of no real change finally led to a major reorganization. For her, this was significantly more painful and more far-reaching than if it had been dealt with earlier.

Ky Nichol raises another interesting issue, which is the impact of process change on technology.

> 'The ability of leadership to adapt business process on the fly is the problem. I was pitching to a major company yesterday, and they were saying, "We want to get process improvement, but it's taking a year to change the systems behind it." The modern worker will just not accept that going forward. Their attitude is, "I'm going to change this particular process within the boundaries I've been given, using my creativity, my insight, and we are going to need to do this by the second, not by the year."'

The challenge then is an organizational one, not necessarily one for employees.

Conclusion

From my interviews, it is clear that process-led transformation is the dominant method deployed. It has a number of key benefits:

- It maintains the perception that it is possible to insulate the rest of the organization from a specific transformation effort in one function or related to one process. The risk of perceived potential distraction in terms of employee performance or customer service can be mitigated.
- The 'end state' is determined upfront and can be linked to a strategic intent. This type of linearity is attractive, as it demonstrates control and predictability of the result.
- Success or failure is easy to determine. The delta between what was conceived and what has been delivered is clear and obvious. The cost of transformation (financial and opportunity costs) are also easy to track.

There are, however, a number of limitations:

▸ From an organizational perspective, the act of insulation and the predetermined end state predicate against any ongoing benefit. There is no incentive for further innovation or change. In fact, the approach positively discriminates against any initiative that may have ancillary benefits but sits outside of the limited risk profile of accountable executives.

▸ Success is based on the capability of senior leadership to devise a strategy that is fit for purpose. With no tolerance for iteration or change as a result of new information, the pressure on leadership to 'get it right' first time is enormous.

This final limitation is something to consider carefully when embarking on a transformation program. It is entirely possible that predicting the future is easier in some sectors than in others. It is also entirely possible that with dedicated experienced resources and little tolerance for variance from a core process, strategic intent and implementation success are completely aligned. These two dimensions are perhaps the core prerequisites for success in process-orientated transformation.

> **Assessing the veracity of these two hypotheses in your organization is an important step.** It will enable you to test whether process-led transformation is the right method for you.

Purpose: Finding a reason to change

The concept of purpose as the primary basis of transformation is challenging. While we as individuals understand and probably have experience of its transformative qualities, the idea that an organization can be purpose-led is difficult to conceptualize. It somehow sits at odds with all the usual perceptions of corporate ambition, be they financial success, market leadership, margins, etc. For us as humans, purpose transcends commerciality. Its power comes from the unambiguous idea that it is a force for good. This is challenging to replicate in a corporate context.

When speaking to interviewees about startups, however, purpose is front and center. It is usually clearly articulated and understood. The rationale is simple. One of the conditions of a purpose-led structure such as a startup is that employees can engage directly with the individual(s) who had the vision. They can interact with the architect and, more importantly, have some influence over future direction. This interaction is key. It keeps the sense of purpose alive and it provides a sense of iteration, which in turn is crucial to get buy-in. One of my interviewees, whom I've referenced earlier, David Heron of WBMS, makes an interesting point when talking about the transformational growth within his own business following a recent private equity investment:

> 'The interesting thing is that as we shift through the gears and I look at what has aligned people to this business more than anything else, it's really clear. Ownership. It makes people accountable. It makes people really care. I have this potentially utopian vision of creating a situation where the business is always owned by the people that are in it and is constantly going through a series of kind of mini MBOs.'

How does it look and feel to be in a purpose-led transformation program?
There are some common characteristics behind purpose-led transformation that are worth exploring. One that is raised frequently is the concept of 'stretch.' This is in the context of a target, a specific aspect of operational or personal performance. How this is expressed varies. There are six examples below:

▸ The effort that individuals put into a process or task because it touches them at a different level from most corporate tasks.

▸ A focus on quality of result where 'good' is not good enough and a person takes it upon him or herself to take the quality of output to a point of excellence.

▸ Deep intellectual curiosity and drive where a problem becomes so absorbing that the person tasked with the solution thinks about it all the time, and where finding a solution becomes a personal thing.

▸ Expected timelines are no longer relevant because of the above commitment. As a result, teams defy expectation and any previous experience to deliver. Through graft and innovation, they meet or exceed expected limitations and time horizons.

▸ The leadership team members change behavior and put themselves at personal risk to achieve something extraordinary. The leadership team shares responsibility as opposed to accountability (the former is proactive, the latter passive). This behavior leads to a sense of humility and authenticity that has viral qualities.

▸ Individuals' personal concerns about their image, positioning, and profile are set aside and they engage fully with those around them, regardless of rank, function, aspiration, and background.

There are a few factors that are kryptonite to the potential power of purpose. At the heart of any purpose-led transformation program is a sense of trust. This is based on a simple principle that the things that motivate and create the environment for extraordinary change are also the things that drive leadership. Mike DeNoma defines this in the idea that any measurement should be a fractal (that is, a measure that is the same for everyone that becomes exponential). If at any stage, there is a sense that these two sets of interests are not aligned, the consequences can be dramatic.

It is difficult, if not impossible, to create a purpose-led transformation program with the following drivers:

▸ Financial performance measures. Creating shareholder value or generating profits are not a motivator to inspire action above and beyond the defined role.
▸ A series of vision statements that are not connected to the actual experience of the employee base. Talking about 'collaboration' when each division or function of your business does not work toward a collective purpose is an example. Focusing on 'engagement' when the primary engagement strategy is an annual electronic survey that has less than 75% participation, and where the actions which arise from it never actually get to implementation, is another.
▸ A product that actively harms your consumer or the environment. This is not a new concept. It is hard to create a sense of purpose that links the individual and their employer when what is being manufactured is known to harm the well-being of the community or society in general.

The long-term impact of purpose-led transformation on employees
Purpose-led transformation has probably had the greatest career impact on my interviewees. For many, programs that have this key element are cited as the best experience of their lives. It is the visualization that they often turn to, in many cases, years after the event.

David Malligan talks about a program of work with Bank Negara in Indonesia (BNI), where he was responsible for bringing more than seven hundred branches of an eight-hundred-branch bank online. Many of these branches were in very remote areas, accessible only by boat. He tells the story of one particular branch on an Island thirteen hours away by boat. In Indonesian terms, this was a small island with a population of around half a million. The primary industries were farming (coconuts), fishing, and mining. The main source of income was money sent home by the youth, who typically left the island at sixteen to eighteen years old to find work or go to university. In the past, the process of sending money home had taken four to six months. Now it was taking four to six seconds.

David relates the conversation:

'It was just this wonderful feeling that you're helping the community. The branch manager, he was in tears. They were able to help all these people, do things immediately when something went wrong or someone was sick, they'd get money to get a doctor, they were able to expand their farm, or they could buy some boats to go fishing. The support that we provided there, that was one of the best moments of my whole career.'

I have covered the Nextel story in detail in the previous chapters, but there is one particular quote which speaks of a similar sentiment from David Cox.

'Our new approach to this customer, the hardworking man / woman, it fundamentally shifted the mindset of the organization from desperately trying to keep our ARPU levels up and extract as much profit to asking the question, "What more can we do for them?" That was the key to creating this kind of inspiration. It was about creating something that had meaning.

What that does is create an inspiring mission that's not about making money. A mission to do something useful in the world. And to connect not only with our customers, but also with the people inside the organization. You're creating that bond, that sense of connection with your customers and with your people. That gives a sense of purpose. That creates this sense of positive energy. We are creating a world where people feel that they're doing something good. We've changed the dialogue from "What can we get out of our customers?"' to '"What can we do for our customers?"'

Kish Gill is a successful corporate financier who spent ten years in investment banking before joining Jardine Matheson, a major conglomerate headquartered in Hong Kong, to take up a CFO role. Kish was seconded to Astra, one of the largest businesses in Southeast Asia, and the largest company in Indonesia, to take up the position of Chief Strategy Officer. He also set up and led a global, group-wide, digital innovation fund initiative for the Jardine Group. Kish left Jardine Matheson / Astra in 2017 to embark on an entrepreneurial journey with the purchase of the Indonesian franchise of Wall Street English, the largest professional English teaching organization in the country.

We had originally arranged our conversation to talk about an innovation lab concept that he was instrumental in introducing at Astra. While that was interesting, the discussion about his new venture, Wall Street English, was really revealing in terms of an approach to transformation that was both insightful and interesting.

Wall Street English is a globally branded and franchised business, established in 1972 with a presence in twenty-eight countries. It is designed to provide a service to all levels of learners, within an English-only environment. In Indonesia, the business had grown steadily with centers primarily on the island of Java.

Post acquisition, and after some time in the centers, Kish saw the need to reset the business model from scratch. His first challenge was a mission, or purpose:

> 'Why do we exist? What's our why as a business? That came pretty easily, to be honest. Our mission is to improve self-confidence, and that's what we're best at in the world, but if that's the case, we have to tweak the way we do business.'

Kish then started to think about the impact on the operational aspect of the business. Wall Street English was going to have to change from selling levels of courses to thinking deeply about the process of making the speaking of English second nature.

> 'You know, in order to dream in English, it's going to have to become part of your life. It's going to have to be a lifestyle. We are going to be a lifestyle business, and what we should be selling therefore is membership. We create communities.'

That approach was clearly going to have an impact on the look and feel of his locations.

> *'I changed them to make them look a lot less like classrooms and a bit more like co-working spaces, where we do all kinds of things from yoga to inviting guest speakers, and where we can talk about current things, like Grab versus GoJek (the two Indonesian equivalents of Uber, but moped-based). We'll have speed-dating events depending on the demographics. Everything's done in English.'*

He then started to think about the buying habits of his customer base, 'millennials.' One of the challenges he recognized very quickly was that this was no longer about selling classes at a specific time, which were only accessible in the center, not remotely. The next step for him was to go digital.

> *'We are going to allow our students to learn through our app on a web-based platform at any time. They're going to be taught by watching a TV series where we have speech recognition. They book in at a time of their convenience at a seminar close to them with one of our native English teachers in a small class. But they can also come to a center at any time to join our daily activities, like a social club, and just hang and speak English.'*

Like the Nextel story, Kish describes an iterative journey of change which is rapid and would have been inconceivable at the point of acquisition. Wall Street English in Indonesia went from selling levels with fixed class schedules and repositioned itself in the lifestyle business to a point where they are building a community around a single purpose. The linkage between building self-confidence and creating fit-for-purpose connections is clear. He gives a few examples:

> *'We have one called "the syndicate," which is focused on businesspeople wanting to practice speaking English. It's to network or to present. We have one called 'Cre-8' which is all about people interested in the arts and talking about fashion.*

The important idea is that when you're talking about something you're passion-ate about, or you talk about a topic you like, you speak naturally. You're not going to think in Bahasa and translate in that immersive environment.

The reality is that a lot of our members find new jobs through their community with us. They make new friends, they learn new things.'

There is a really interesting nuance here. The new sense of purpose and direction, coupled with a fresh perspective of customer need, completely changed the business operating model. The driver for change is purpose, not strategic rationale.

What about the transformation journey, what do we learn?

It will not be a surprise to anyone who has embarked on this type of transformational change that the biggest challenge is changing people's mindsets. Kish describes it well:

'People who have been here a long time, they find it the hardest. "We are used to doing things a certain way, and now you're telling them that what we're selling is membership? Or community?"

We're changing everything. Sales consultants became personal solutions consultants, receptionists became mentors, teachers became trainers, their job isn't to teach, actually, they facilitate learning. And then we have started recruiting based on personality. We don't recruit the trainers based on how good they are as a teacher, but on how engaging their personalities and characters are. Your competency is important, but what we care about is your being able to project yourself in an authentic and honest way about who you are.'

What was the impact of that kind of radical change?

'I've had virtually 80% employee turnover, which was intentional. It's my own money; I can't wait around for people to get their heads around the new direction. I'm going to hire people who believe in my mission, who believe in this new direction, and we'll go from there.

I've had to change a lot of people and do a lot of culture-building again. I'm very focused on making sure my employees believe in this logic, that they're not doing this just for the money. We're doing this to change people's lives. We're doing this to make Indonesia a more competitive country and its people much more competitive.'

What about the results?

Wall Street English Indonesia has gone through a complete remodeling of its centers over the past eighteen months. Each new center has a look and feel that reflects the new operating model.

In terms of NPS, the company is first in Asia in terms of customer satisfaction.

Some center sales are up 30% year on year for the last seven months or so. The business has been growing by 15% to 40% per month and has been cashflow positive for the last seven months.

How has he personally found the change?

'It's very, very hard work. You need to drink a lot of your own Kool-Aid. I'm a finance guy so this doesn't come naturally.

The big thing has been the culture building. When I looked at this opportunity first as an investment opportunity, I looked at it from an Excel file, right? I raised money and put the deck together for it. It was all based on our standard M&A analysis...the returns, if you exit at this multiple in five years' time, these are the projections. I think we can do X number of cents of growth, etc., I thought from an operational perspective, I will sort out the licenses and bring in the native teachers and do more of the same and it'll all be fine. And I never expected that I would have to learn by myself how to get people engaged around a certain mission. That was a piece that doesn't come to me naturally.'

What's been the impact on him?

'I have no regrets really. I miss having a regular paycheck. I miss the intellectual banter. I don't get to meet those kinds of people anymore. And it's pretty

*lonely sometimes when you don't have a board that you can talk to and bounce
ideas off.'*

Postscript

I caught up with Kish recently to find out how things were progressing and how
COVID-19 had affected the business. He confirmed the extraordinary growth prior
to March 2020 with twenty-two months of consecutive year-on-year growth. COVID-
19 forced a rapid re-think in terms of digital innovation and delivery, in response to
a different type of demand from customers, but also reflecting the lack of support
from government for businesses in general. Wall Street English successfully
changed its business model over the period, and thrived. He comments:

> *'As a result, our sales and profitability are higher than ever before, and we are
> now accelerating our growth out of this pandemic. I believe that we are the
> only cash flow positive and profitable edtech business in Indonesia.'*

Wall Street English is an interesting story. The way Kish tells it shows the ups and
downs of implementation. It shows the real strength of 'purpose-led' transformation. It shows the incredible potential when a team is really motivated. There is a
refreshing candor about his motivation and his challenges that rings true with many
of my interviewees.

Kish's story is that of the classic entrepreneur, albeit with an interesting twist re
motive and purpose. He clearly has commercial interests, but recognizes that
achieving those results is about so much more than a balance-sheet exercise.

Focus and decision making

How does purpose-led transformation work with more established founder-led
businesses with customers, employees, supply chains, etc.?

One of the distinguishing characteristics of these businesses is their ability to cut
through bureaucracy in their speed of decision making and provide a laser-like focus
for the transformation program. It is tempting to attribute this to the fact that the
capital being spent is still in part their own. I suspect, however, that once the attri-

butes of focus and speed of decision making are established and proven, they live in the minds of all employees and are remarkably resilient.

An ex-colleague from PwC, Ben Lazarus, tells just such a story. Ben is a post-merger integration expert, with a depth of global experience that is matched only by his humility. In this case, he is describing a merger of equals between a Middle Eastern and a North American Hi-Tech company with combined revenues of circa $700m, experiencing hyper growth of around 20-40% annually. Both were highly entrepreneurial but culturally very different. He describes one particular interaction between the two sales teams to demonstrate the cultural difference:

> 'The two sales teams were asked to present their business. One lot stood up and gave a fact-driven PowerPoint presentation. It included KPIs on leads and opportunities closed and won, gates, levels of business. The other team had no presentation; they talked about the depth of their relationships with their customers.'

I asked him about the general attitude to the deal:

> 'There was a lot of skepticism; people were very comfortable in their world, but there was high degree of trust in the existing leadership, more than we see in many mergers. But that trust had to be gained in this deal.'

And how was that trust won? What were the factors involved?

> In the kick-off meeting, two things happened that worked really well. The two CEOs developed and gave a very coherent strategy and clear understanding of "where we want to be—an X-million dollar business within two years, and what it is going to take to do it." They gave a very clear picture, and we addressed culture from the very start.'

In terms of implementation, how did that level of focus manifest itself?

> 'There were two things...first, decisions were made quickly. A lot of decisions that would have bogged down other organizations were resolved fast...decisions like the name of the company, the top team, do we follow Model A or

> *Model B, which systems to take, what commission rates to offer resellers...*
> *these were all resolved fast.'*

This is an interesting response. The examples he gives are mostly operational, and as a result enable the integration to maintain its pace while also allowing 'business as usual' to continue without pause. The leadership of the business was clearly one where 'command and control' is the prevailing management approach, but they are brave enough to realize that with this comes the pressure to respond fast. There is a close alignment between the operational requirements of the business and the leadership team's priorities.

> *'The second thing was that teams were not siloed. The main reason for the*
> *acquisition was about cross-selling. We created an 'order to fulfillment' work*
> *stream that included sales, marketing, branding, customer support, customer*
> *service, finance. The objective was to get cross-selling moving as fast as*
> *possible. The understanding was that we weren't going to wait for a happy*
> *marriage of ERP delivery...the question we decided to address was what each*
> *function needed to do to be agile and get out the door as quickly as possible*
> *to start cross-selling.'*

At the heart of Ben's story are some clear characteristics: pragmatism, clarity of purpose, speed of response, fairness, and engagement. They also happen to be the characteristics for successful purpose-led transformation.

Is there a downside to purpose-led transformation?

Is it possible to identify a situation where your sense of purpose can actually get in the way of a transformation program? A situation where deeply held beliefs become a blocker to change?

There are situations where being purpose-led becomes a constraint, reinforcing behaviors that are not helpful in transformation.

One of those behaviors is risk aversion.

Martin Hodgson was CEO of a specialist global program and project management business called PCUBED prior to its sale to Mi GSO. His background in program management is broad. He has worked in the automotive sector with Ford and Jaguar Land Rover as portfolio and program director on transformation programs in the UK and internationally. He has also worked in the UK public sector. Martin describes a very significant program of work with the Metropolitan Police (the Met) in London. The program was initiated to deliver significant cost savings with no material impact on service. Maintaining reputation during the process was critical. With a cost base of around 90% people costs, the program had the potential of generating all the wrong headlines.

Martin describes the culture as follows:

'You've got this odd mix of things that are actually great for driving change effectively and things which are a real blockage to change. There is a real passion for doing the right thing, being prepared to look at things and the way they work openly. There is a willingness to face up to bad news and deal with it honestly. They're used to working in a mess, every situation they go into, they're expecting things not to work. So when that happens, they're ready for it and their reactions are fantastic. Those are the great things about the Met.

There are some real blind spots too. They're so risk averse. You just don't change things there if there's a risk. And given their track record in technology, which is terrible but probably one of the only drivers for cost effective operational improvement, it's hard to change things there.'

It is an interesting situation. For the Met, risk aversion is a critical part of the institutional culture. It sits at the heart of an organization in which the safety of the public is the essential purpose. The problem is that it is all-pervasive. Delivering change without risk is hard to do.

The constraints and challenges of a shared experience

The bond that's established between team members in periods of stress, squeezed timelines, and limited resources is powerful and fulfilling. For many program managers, this is the endorphin rush and the primary reason for continuing to work in the world of transformation.

Shared experiences are perhaps one of the most common ways to establish a purpose-led business. Purpose is, by its very nature, collective and collaborative. The 'rite of passage' for the military in going through basic training together, or for the Metropolitan Police in starting 'on the beat' are two examples in the public sector. Similar experiences exist in certain private-sector companies. Starting work at the bottom, whether that's in a retail store or a call center, provides a similar sense of shared experience. Contact with the customer from day one is core to that shared experience.

The ability for these businesses to grow while maintaining this shared experience and the culture that it creates is constrained by the ability to recruit, retain, and promote these resources. The choice is a difficult one...compromise on the shared experience for your employees and grow with demand, or protect the culture and grow at a slower pace.

This challenge is illustrated in the story from a senior UK-based program director, with more than fifteen years' experience in the automotive and retail sectors around the world. He described a program to introduce an online 'Ratings and Review' capability for a well-known furniture manufacturer and retailer. This organization had a very strong culture based on a set of ethics that led to a distinctive approach with regard to profit sharing, sustainability, and the impact on the environment.

Ratings and Reviews was an early initiative to enable customers to rate and review products. It recognized the concept that other customers would respond well to an 'independent' evaluation of their products. It also recognized that in enabling this type of public / social media commentary, the business was creating a bond with its customers.

Ratings and Reviews was a new concept for this organization. In particular, the idea that the company would be exposing the quality of its products via social media with little control was a big leap. The possibility that their product range might be influenced by external reviewers and data was a major change. The potential impact of large, external, 'independent' data sets that might not necessarily concur with the internal perspective was challenging, politically and culturally.

It was recognized, however, that for a new generation of customers, feedback and responsiveness were two critical parts of building a relationship of trust. Given that much of the design took place in-house, this immediate type of feedback had the potential of being very valuable.

The real implementation challenge?

It became clear fairly quickly that establishing a powerful external review process and system was not the actual implementation challenge.

The main issue was, in fact, that the idea was being driven by managers and employees who had not had the same shared experience of working on the shop floor. Furthermore, most of the members of this group were based in some of the newest localities around the world. There was a perception that they were not part of the core legacy.

The program quickly began to experience some of the classic difficulties that arise from a lack of engagement and trust in what the outcome might be:

▸ Accessing existing data was a challenge. Data owners were reluctant to release information.
▸ Attendance at steering committee meetings was sparse, and meetings were often disrupted. The program was not seen as a priority.
▸ Credibility and the potential benefits of the program were regularly challenged. A restatement of benefits became necessary at most meetings.

These challenges to the program were disruptive. They had the potential for delay and further obfuscation. The response from the program team needed to be powerful. The following actions were taken:

▸ A document outlining the purpose, benefits, and timeline of the program was published with the signatures of every senior director. Buy-in was now explicit, not implicit.
▸ All documentation, reporting, and status reports were published and made accessible to all through the internal intranet. The program operated with complete transparency, a core tenet of the company's culture.
▸ Pilots were run in a series of countries, and the results were shared.

▸ A third party was engaged to manage the inputs from customers, with a quick turnaround from input to publishing. This maintained the concept of 'independence.'

▸ Data was shared with designers and other teams. One of the early outcomes was an increase in the speed of response. This materialized in two ways: commercial policy (discounting heavily products that were not well reviewed, and being open about the reason in-store and online), and responding very quickly to any challenge with regard to sourcing of materials.

What is perhaps most interesting about this program was its long-term effect across the organization. The Ratings and Review program led to a radical review of culture, people change management, and knowledge sharing to reflect the changing, maturing nature of the business.

It is a good example of how purpose-led change is not constrained by any functional or structural silos but has a much broader impact.

Conclusion

In this chapter I have quoted extensively from four stories: Wall Street English, the merger of two hi-tech businesses, BNI, and the global furniture manufacturer.

Beyond the purpose-led nature of their transformation programs, it is hard to find anything similar in any of these four case studies. All the normal dimensions of geography, size and scale, industry, age, marketplace, and ambition are fundamentally different.

Their transformation challenges are equally different. In the case of Wall Street English, the challenge is one of building a startup that has the potential to change perception. In the case of BNI, the transformation feels like a public service that is related to its mission and ownership structure. In the case of the furniture manufacturer, the task itself is relatively contained and clearly articulated, but the ramifications are much bigger, and these start to appear as the implementation develops.

No end state…and no limitations
There is, however, one theme that seems to emerge from these stories. That is that there is no point of completion!

How does that happen? For a start, the outcomes are less well defined than they are in process-led change. Enabling and getting the benefit of a broad coalition of effort and innovation leads to continuous change. Leadership's ability to confine the context and impact of the transformation program disappears.

Why? First, if the purpose of the organization changes in response to the needs of a customer, or the climate (as two examples), then the transformation program will follow.

Second, internal interpretation of required change will evolve as the employee base evolves. What was acceptable in previous years in terms of a corporate response to climate change, for example, is no longer adequate. This is in part because of the quality of information and perceived urgency of necessary action. It is also, however, because the expectations of a new generation of employee are considerably greater in terms of what can and what should be done.

If you lead an organization that has a strong sense of purpose, it is likely that you will attract others who can relate to this and will want to influence the direction of travel.

Third, precisely because a broad coalition of employees has been engaged, the potential to constrain the program becomes more challenging, if not impossible. The transformation effort becomes an organic one, irrespective of budget, governance, or structure. It becomes part of the DNA of the business. For purpose-led change, defining a 'north star' and then leaving the organization to self-manage and evolve has the consequence of continuous evolution.

No 'entry' requirements

In this chapter I have given four examples, and I could have included many more. Purpose-led transformation capability would appear to be something that, with authentic leadership, employee engagement, and empathetic leadership is available to all.

Plasticity: Transformation is the 'DNA'

If Process and Purpose are the lungs of this book, then Plasticity is the heart. There is an interdependence, but there is also a core. Above, I defined plasticity as being a prerequisite for any transformation program. Any organization going through a transformation needs to adopt some of the characteristics of plasticity. This is true whether it is in the context of a purpose-led, company-wide program or a process-led transformation that is looking to change a specific activity or process.

The challenge, when trying to translate any concept from the world of science into the world of business, is that the definition rests in the mind of the author, not in the mind of the reader. I need to change the pronoun of 'my' idea of plasticity to 'our' idea of plasticity. As in previous chapters, the main focus here will be case studies and experiences that will hopefully correspond with some of your own.

According to Merriam-Webster, 'plasticity' has three distinct but related definitions:

1. the quality or capacity of being molded or altered.
2. the ability to retain a shape attained by pressure deformation.
3. the capacity of organisms with the same genotype to vary in developmental pattern, in phenotype, or in behavior, according to varying environmental conditions.

We are all familiar with the first two. The last one is intriguing, however, and no less relevant. The concept that an organism or organization can change while maintaining the same genotype corresponds well with the idea that wholesale change of a culture does not require wholesale change in terms of employees, processes, and systems.

Thinking, then, about the properties of plasticity in the context of a company, how might one define those? I have set out three ideas below:

First, 'agility' or the idea of 'agile' in transformation. 'Agile' is a process of implementation in which small, self-organizing teams iterate the components of design, develop, and test in very short time frames, with very frequent engagement with the customer and other stakeholders.

This means that scope is also iterative as the teams explore and develop different solutions to the complex problem they are trying to resolve, in partnership with the customer. The challenge for 'agile' is that it requires the entire organization to recognize this different way of working.

In traditional program / project management practice, there are four core components that need to be agreed upon very early in the process. These are the scope of the work, the cost of implementation, the time required to complete, and the quality of output that is required.

In an 'agile' program, none of these elements can be agreed upon at inception. Each will iterate as the solution develops. This is difficult for most organizations. The constant review of strategy through implementation, which is what is required in an 'agile' program, is counterintuitive for most companies and leadership teams. For them, strategy leads and implementation follows. The traditional approach requires a definition of 'where we're going *before* we can define how we get there.'

As David Lowe describes it, that idea is based on an idea that needs to be challenged:

> *'Organizations often ask for things believing that the world is simple and predictable.'*

The value of agility is that it recognizes that our forecasting ability is often limited and based on too few or the wrong data points. It is also based on an idea that implementation is linear once direction has been set. As we've seen in the previous chapters, that is far from the truth.

The second key concept for organizations that have plasticity is the idea of 'adaptability.' While it is entirely expected that the teams that are tasked with delivering the transformation display the qualities of plasticity, it is important that the rest of the organization also responds. Some examples of where this is particularly important:

▸ Core corporate functions such as HR, Finance, Technology, and Operations need to adapt to become enablers, not definers of scope. What they deliver is directly linked to the requirements of the overall transformation objective. This objective cannot be constrained by the context and limitations of the scope of their own functional leadership teams. If these constraints exist, they need to be challenged and changed.

- Policies and processes need to adapt to the current demands of the organization. This change has to be proactive, fast, and continuous. Their role is to provide an immediate set of guide rails to current and future risks and challenges. Two things need to happen quickly: the first is to identify owners who are accountable for specific processes and policies; the second is to move from a base of retrospective policy and process based on past learnings to responding quickly and pragmatically to current and future requirements. It is worth remembering that this might be as much about radically reducing policies and processes as it might be about adding more.

- Resourcing (capital and human) needs to adapt to immediate short requirements. The strategy for resourcing has to be reviewed on a real-time basis. The boundaries between fixed and flexible workforce have been blurred for a while, reflecting a continued focus on reducing fixed cost. Creating flexible resource pools (either within the outsourced provider) or by developing a workforce internally that can change to respond to the immediate requirements are two ideas to consider.

- Leadership behaviors and ways of working change need to adapt to the needs of the program. This is closely aligned to the concept of strategy and implementation constantly iterating. It is also driven by both rational and psychological demands as the employee base begins to experience change. Adaptability in this context does not mean 'insulation' arising from security based on reward and guaranteed continued tenure but real change based on the experiences of those involved in the transformation. There has been much written with regard to the need for 'authenticity' of leadership in change. If the impact of what is being proposed is allowed to be limited to non-leadership roles, the opportunity for authentic leadership is lost.

The third key concept is 'responsiveness.' I have touched on pace already. This is part of the new-found adaptability that organizations need to nurture. The concept stands well on its own, however. Changing the pace of decision making and escalating risks and opportunities all lead to collective behavioral change. Changing the pace does not imply constantly faster, by the way. It needs to be appropriate for the current situation.

There is a final dimension to consider in thinking about the properties of plasticity, and that is 'alignment' between goals and implementation process. In other words, the transformation process needs to be authentic to the transformation goal. If one of the core principles to reach for is greater trust, 'measuring' performance in a fashion which suggests a lack of trust will kill the implementation process in its entirety.

What are the key drivers that lead to plasticity in organizations?

As already mentioned, process and purpose are two access points to achieving plasticity in an organization. They are, however, not the only ones. There are other situations that almost force an organization into a state of plasticity.

The 'It is too complicated for our collective brains to understand' driver

All of us will have been in situations where this dynamic is at play. Even as we try to think about the issue and deploy whatever resource we can access, the task seems to have too many moving parts.

For the motivated team that has some kind of collaborative spirit, the response is often a simple one. 'Let's just start doing stuff!' it is important to recognize that that 'stuff' is not random, however. It is a process of positive enquiry including iterative, discovery conversations with different subject matter experts and innovative, left-brained people. The process of mapping output is also interesting to note. For many, mind mapping is the tool of choice. For others it might be drawing pictures. For yet others, it is coming up with an increasingly honed form of words or a description to capture the essence of the challenge.

This process does not follow any governance structure. Meetings are almost always 'standup,' with no fixed agenda but with a firm, collective desire to reach a decision and the next step. At its absolute core, the process is iterative.

One of my interviewees is a senior project manager with a seasoned background in the investment and commercial banking sector. He started his career in the Middle Office, the link between the trading desks and the operations area, before moving into project and program management. His story is a fascinating insight from a program management perspective into the most radical regulatory change to hit the investment banking sector in a hundred years.

The context was the 2008 financial crisis and the response by regulators around the world to that threat to the global financial system. What emerged became known as the Volcker Rule. The main purpose of this was to regulate the reporting and conditions under which traders were allowed to take proprietary positions, by limiting the amount of risk a trader can take. This was based on an assessment of what size position a customer might take in certain market conditions. The rule was captured in a hundred pages of regulatory language and a thousand pages of guidance. It applied to any bank with a US entity or presence, to all intents and purposes making it a 'global' regulation.

The regulation was particularly challenging because it required a change in trading behavior. Any breach required immediate escalation, with all the usual sanctions of fines and potential prison sentences for those directly implicated.

Looking at the implementation of the program, the team started to see all sorts of challenges, specifically around scope. This is how my interviewee describes the start of the program:

> 'There was this huge amount of legal effort, SMEs getting involved, industry bodies getting involved, cross sector committees, industry forums, just to interpret what it really meant. You'd expect with a thousand pages of guidance the regulation would be very prescriptive. But actually it was just very theoretical. We realized after a while that it wasn't telling us anything about what we needed to do differently. We needed to define it completely to see how this was going to work within our business.
>
> The reality was that even the regulators didn't know what implementation was going to look like. When we asked for feedback once we were in implementation mode, what we got back was vague and very non-committal.'

He then goes on to talk about the approach the team adopted in terms of program management:

> 'At the start of the program it was so ill defined that we had no idea of what we were actually going to do. There was zero focus on plan, on risks and issues.

It was a group of people, sitting down together, recognizing that we, this little group around the table, have got to get this done.

The team sort of fell into two relatively distinct groups, not that we proactively organized ourselves in that way. Those that just went out and got shit done and the others who tried to create a wrapper around it to make it look like a program from the outside. It started off as not quite chaos, but people going and having conversations being theoretical, trying to get people engaged, all of that stuff, not caring about any of the project stuff, no budgeting, no nothing, no one cared about any of that.

It was only halfway through the project that there was more focus on the streams. At that stage we were doing governance and status reporting at a relatively granular level across trading desks and then across to the regulatory function.'

We talked about existing methods of managing complex programs with the bank, as to whether these ever really featured in the process. Most global banks are process-oriented in terms of any transformation program and prescriptive in terms of any program management process. His response took me by surprise.

'There was never a moment where the "This is the way we run projects" discussion took place. It was, "We will do what we need to do to get this over the line." The best way to report on status is this, the best way to plan is that. The best way to look at governance for this deliverable is this rather than taking some "off the shelf type" things. There was never any challenge to that either.'

His response to the 'elegant, silver bullet' solution and what was actually delivered is also interesting to capture:

'At the outset we were maybe a bit optimistic about how much we might be able to automate some of what was required. We thought that technology was going to help us. Actually the solution was much more tactical. In hindsight that was definitely the right approach.'

To summarize: for the most complex, radical piece of regulatory change in living memory to have hit a sector where the punishment for noncompliance was being sent to prison, the team in charge of implementation for one of the largest banks in the world got to a point of delivery where the ultimately highly successful implementation approach was to ignore all that wonderful theory around plans, etc., and deliver through constant, fast, and very tactical iteration...'doing stuff'!

Note also that the barriers for change, the parts of the organization that would normally require adherence to procedures and processes, no longer intervene. For the period of the transformation, the organization, its structures and functions adapt and respond to the needs of the program.

Starting with implementation, retro-fitting strategy

Over the past thirty years we have started to see situations where a groundswell of opinion can radically change a perceived status quo. The most eye-catching of these have been political change.

The second example of a driver that sits outside of process and purpose is one where the impetus for change is organization-wide and becomes viral. It is only broadly defined or rarely planned at senior or functional leadership level. In this situation, the iteration between strategy and implementation becomes seamless. Implementation informs strategy.

Iterating scope and 'no blame'

Another feature of plasticity is that its explicit requirement for collaboration extends to unplanned scope change. This is different from the examples we have seen from a process-led transformation approach where scope change is perceived as a threat and therefore rejected. One of the insights from the interviews is that when an implementation team is functioning well there is a sense that nothing can stop it from delivering successfully, even if it comes to identifying significant additional scope during delivery. This acceptance and embrace of more things to do is remarkable and counterintuitive.

Mark Beeden is a senior financial services program director with more than twelve years' experience in the UK and international banking market. His background in operations and business change was the starting point for a long career in program management, but in the last few years regulatory driven change has become his primary area of specialization.

Mark's story comes from the period post 2008 financial crisis. Globally, financial services regulators were focused on minimizing the potential for systemic collapse. This resulted in the development of a ring-fencing requirement. Every bank in the UK with activities from investment to retail banking was charged with the responsibility of building a ring-fenced retail bank. This business needed to be able to operate entirely independently, in terms of people, process, and systems, from any other part of the business in the event of another global crisis.

Mark's inflection point on the program came after he had been in place for six months. He describes the moment:

> 'One of the lead architects on the program calls me into an urgent meeting. His opening line is, "Someone's forgotten to move the data. We don't have anyone looking at how we get the client reference data into the new systems. We think we've missed it entirely."
>
> Not only that, no one had a clue how to move it. Our program was about getting the system set up to accept new clients into the bank, but there was a whole world of other programs that are doing transferring trades, for example. Not one of them had considered how they would get the client data into any of their systems, either.
>
> The second thing that became clear was that no one knew the data architecture. We had to map out the data flows in the bank. That was quite a shocking reality check. No idea about data flows, data points, none of it.'

The scale of this omission is dramatic. Each bank has literally millions of clients with millions of trades. The data is held in legacy systems where data quality is extremely suspect. In many cases the legacy systems were extraordinarily bespoke as a result of continued change over many years. The architects or owners of these systems have often retired. Understanding the systems and then migrating the data was an enormous undertaking.

So what happened next?

> 'It was the moment where we as a team sat down and recognized we had to do this. We said to leadership, give us the resources and we will do this. Everyone came together. As a team we recognized that if this fails, we all fail.'

It is worth noting that the initial reaction was not one of blame, of trying to identify who had failed to scope the program correctly. The sense that no issue was too difficult to solve comes across very clearly.

That positivity is not an isolated instance. In the story about the Volcker Rule program, a similar event took place.

> 'There was one part of the regulation that we had thought was pretty minor. Our subject matter experts agreed. We also thought it would be easy to solve. We were definitely over halfway when it transpired that that aspect was a lot bigger and a lot more complicated than we thought it was going to be. Interestingly, there wasn't any finger pointing at the time in terms of why this wasn't picked up.'

We have no choice

This third example is related to the 'too complex to deal with' concept, but it also addresses a situation where there is no alternative. A moment where the fundamental economics of the business are being challenged. In the Nextel case study, one gets a strong sense of the power that existential threat has on behavior and attitudes to change. In this next example, the threat is not existential and the impact of noncompliance on employees is perhaps less radical. The threat is industry-changing none the less.

The example below comes from an interview with a head of portfolio with over twenty years' experience running complex transformation programs across a range of sectors across Southeast Asia.

The context to our conversation was that of an industry going through significant change. The driver for this was predominantly economic.

This shift from its current positioning led to a major change in terms of organizational structure, decision making, governance, and behavior change. At the heart of this transformation was a commitment to moving toward a more agile-based business: one focused on building networks and enabling the evolution of self-organizing teams. The initiative had been borrowed from two prominent businesses from outside the sector: Spotify and ING. The transformation touched all parts of the business.

The framework above demonstrated some of the unique aspects of the sector, in particular with the lack of integration between customer needs and innovation. As part of a clear direction from the CEO, customer experience was going to be part of this new vision, specifically in the process of providing better and more coordinated access to the product portfolio from the perspective of key information and guidance.

What are the key steps in this process of transformation?
My interviewee describes a series of significant changes:

▸ First, with regard to the organizational structure and the authority matrix, the organization has embarked on a process of radical decentralization, where decision making has been forced downwards to affiliate (country) level. The organizational structure that used to exist between the center and these local organizations has been totally dismantled. The leaderships of more than a hundred companies now report into one head.
▸ Where there are intermediary roles, their roles are specifically not about decision making and leadership, but about coaching, mentoring, and a positive challenge about direction in regard to the 'north star.'
▸ The lack of management direction has created an environment where the affiliates are forced to collaborate with each other, in terms of sharing best practice, scaling where required, and establishing consistent processes where it is valuable to do so.

What are the key challenges?
He describes the issues well:

'This is not a startup where you can hire those who fit into this structure. We have existing archetypes, people, in other words, who need to change to fit into the new world. That is why the journey is interesting but equally challenging.

I'm a good example of that. I have spent my career doing 90% value maintenance work and I'm being asked to reverse that completely to 90% value creation, which, by the way, I have to define myself. That involves my working with my colleagues in a completely different way where we are co-creating those opportunities and how we measure them personally and as a team.

When I'm working with some colleagues from different markets, the conversation has changed. I can give guidance where in the past I've given direction. It's painful for both of us, but it is critical to build this kind of bottom-up, empowered, ownership behavior that we need going forward.'

How is the transformation working out?

'The transformation remains a work in progress. There continues to be resistance internally, however the direction of travel is irreversible.'

These struggles are a great example of the challenges of introducing plasticity into an organization that has been stable and consistent for a long time, in a sector that does not change very much. The way in which R&D is done in this environment does not just reflect a commercial, operational norm, it is also a by-product of the educational infrastructure and culture that many of the employees have experienced prior to joining. Intellectual rigor, robust peer review, testing...these are all hallmarks of a science based education. While these dimensions are not being challenged in the new environment, the requirement for continuous iteration, involving all the different stakeholders, is undoubtedly different.

Plasticity in the 'real' world

Exploring the idea of plasticity with my interviewees and network is one thing, but understanding how to implement is quite another. While road testing the concept of plasticity among a group of M&A practitioners at the HR M&A Roundtable Conference in 2020, the question of measurement was raised. Is it possible to measure how 'plastic' an organization is? Are there indicators that might give leadership a view? What would those indicators look like?

There are two questions to deal with here. First, in the same spirit of what gets measured gets done, can we put a rational performance value to plasticity, and can we benchmark ourselves internally or eventually externally? Second, is there a correlation between transformation success and plasticity that might inform leadership decisions of resourcing, capital, etc.?

I am going to respond to both of these challenges in turn.

What are the indicators that illustrate the presence of plasticity in my business?

Let us imagine that our only access point to the organization is a virtual data room. For those not familiar with a due diligence process, this is an online facility where information on a target acquisition is stored and made accessible for the acquirer. It often runs to many thousands of different documents.

Let me divide the indicators into three groups: People, Processes, and Systems.

People:

Organizations with plasticity have much less rigidity in terms of the boundaries between functions and business units. Careers, influence, and hierarchy are not defined in the context of role description but more in the adaptability and responsiveness to organizational need and market opportunity.

How does that look from a data room, desk top review process, therefore?

▸ Movement of people across functions is frequent and unremarkable. At the top of the organization, leadership roles are typically filled from within and from different disciplines. Elsewhere, mid and senior level management roles have a similar profile, and the selection process demonstrates an agnostic perspective with regard to previous internal experience.

▸ Functions appear or disappear frequently, and their descriptions / titles and what they do change. Individuals running them may stay constant, but it is clear that they are being measured with different objectives.

Processes:

A similar trend exists in terms of processes. Process change is constant and frequent. Processes are recognized as enablers for change. They are not activities that have an indefinite and undeniable right to exist. Workflow mapping is driven by either operational efficiency, growth, and its impact on processing capability, or by a new customer or other externally driven requirement.

In terms of the data room challenge then, what might you find?

▸ As part of any operational efficiency initiative, a review of existing processes, the adoption of new processes, and the regular challenge and dropping of legacy processes that are no longer fit for purpose.
▸ Frequent process change exists across all functions.
▸ The documentation for process change is pragmatic, consistent, and easy to read. It is internally driven and internally sponsored at a senior level (there is no dependency on external consultants to deliver this change).

Systems:

As with processes, systems change is constant and frequent.

▸ Systems change occurs frequently, with new applications being added to the tech platform every year.
▸ The role of systems architect is well established and explicitly recognizes the need for streamlining systems as well as adding additional capability.
▸ The architecture artefact is relatively easy to understand and has been communicated across the organization frequently.

How does it feel when you're in an organization that has plasticity?

The next section, about ecosystems, describes some of the characteristics of organizations with plasticity, but it is worth noting some of the themes that emerge from my interviews here.

The first is positivity. At the heart of a successful change program and specifically within an organization that is adapting in a self-organizing, anticipatory type of way, is an overwhelming sense of positivity. The employees within this environment enjoy the experience and appear to approach each new challenge with relish. There is an element of the concept that artists, authors, musicians, and surgeons describe as 'flow,' where the task becomes fully immersive and the individuals involved are energized by the process. A side-effect of this type of immersion is that working and nonworking hours are no longer distinguishable. This is not about time spent in the office but the discretionary time that we can choose to dedicate to whichever activity gives us the most fulfillment.

The second is individual accountability. This is not about accountability that has been forced upon the individual, but rather accountability that the individual has asked for and is held tight.

The third is a lightness of spirit; some might describe it as fun. Even in the most remedial of situations, it seems that humor prevails and has an important part to play in bringing the organization together and creating a bond across functions, hierarchies, locations, and activities.

Conclusion

The key challenge in this chapter has been to demonstrate that plasticity is not just an outcome of a successful purpose or process-driven transformation program, but that there are in fact programs of change that have a different, 'organic' origin that sits deep within the business. The driver for this type of change may be loosely connected to some 'north star' or vision, but that the distance between that and implementation is so great that some level of self-organization fills the vacuum. This process is not based on a methodology or model, but is repeatable, using the mental muscle memory of those involved and creating the right environment where the core components of that muscle memory are encouraged to prosper.

Enabling plasticity to exist in your organization, then, is not something that happens by chance. It requires a mixture of proactive behavior change and the right environment or ecosystem. It is the latter that I'm going to explore next.

04
THE 'ECOSYSTEM' BEHIND GOOD TRANSFORMATION: CREATING AN ENVIRONMENT TO ENABLE CHANGE

Throughout this book there have been examples of successful transformation in a variety of industries and geographies. Sectors and location are factors that have an impact on the unique nature of each program.

But what of the companies themselves? What impact does the corporate ecosystem (as defined earlier as an amalgam of social infrastructure and processes / systems) have on transformation? Is a good ecosystem enough on its own to enable successful transformation programs?

It seems sensible to break down some of the components that sit behind a 'transformation-friendly' ecosystem and examine each on their merits.

A note before we get into the examples. This chapter draws on the experience of external advisers and specifically mergers and acquisitions. Mergers and acquisitions provide the conditions that demonstrate 'good' and 'bad' in terms of ecosystem most clearly. The flexibility, responsiveness, and decision-making characteristics of organizations involved in a deal are laid bare in a way that is hard to hide internally and externally.

Let's talk about culture

Diagnostic, diagnostic, diagnostic!
Everywhere you look these days, the wish to describe culture is all pervasive, probably as a response to the famous Peter Drucker quote, 'Culture eats strategy for breakfast.' Interestingly, finding the source of that particular quote is difficult.

Sadly, what we find in terms of culture programs in transformation is a lot of techniques around diagnosis but not much else. There is a fundamental problem with this approach, as David Boyd says:

> *'Culture diagnostics are a little like the moment when the hairdresser shows you the back of your head using a mirror...fascinating, but there's bugger-all you can do about it at that stage.'*

What is the problem, then, with moving beyond the diagnostic? Why are we still focused on the problem and not the solution?

I suspect the problem is pretty simple...for such big ideas, the most successful solutions are very small and not particularly eye-catching!

- ▸ Removing the doors from the C-Suite's offices is extremely impactful for those who sit in their vicinity and sends a powerful message, but it's hardly rocket science.
- ▸ Introducing 'back to the floor' initiatives for senior leadership where they actually spend time in call centers or in production facilities or on the road with sales teams is extremely powerful as a learning exercise, but not particularly popular, and hard to enforce.
- ▸ Changing floor plans in an insurance company so that those who sell policies and those who handle claims sit next to each other works well as a method of broadening client interaction and engagement, but is challenging for both the individuals who are involved and the Property / IT team who are the enablers.
- ▸ Focusing on really small behavioral traits at the leadership level (time keeping / asking more questions than giving answers / walking the floors) requires a combination of a great relationship and courage based on a coaching aspiration...not easy for anyone internal to develop.

▶ Bringing together the loud, articulate, often critical but highly regarded team members to resolve meaningful internal and external challenges takes time, iteration, and patience, but the results can be spectacular...ignoring them is much easier!

▶ Following through on innovation lab recommendations ensuring that those who have put forward ideas get to write business plans / implementation plans and are involved in delivery (successful or otherwise). That is where the real value of the initiative sits...not in the 'messaging behind the initiative.'

▶ For the CEO to spend the next three months focusing on customer engagement scores (and nothing else) within every meeting that he or she holds to create a focus on this across all functions is hardly challenging as a concept, but potentially groundbreaking for the business.

None of these are extraordinary, but I have seen all of them produce extraordinary results.

Macro or micro? Where does corporate culture actually exist?

The other major issue is that of scale. Whenever we talk about culture, it's almost always in macro-economic terms...regions, nations, industries, functional areas all seem to be easily (if often wrongly) defined by specific and identifiable cultural traits. These traits enable us to ascribe labels to groups of people that may be relevant in terms of description. In terms of achieving any kind of change, however, they add to the confusion rather than reduce it.

What emerges from the interviews is something altogether more micro. I have divided the findings into the following three key themes:

▶ The actual cultural dimension that matters to an individual is that of his or her immediate surroundings. No matter how centralized or controlled the organization might be, the way that work is conducted is determined by a lower to middle (in terms of hierarchy) layer of leadership.

▶ This layer of leadership is not 'permafrost,' as it has been defined in the past, but rather a much more flexible, plastic material. It actually consists of every possible version of leader: the young, highly motivated, inexperienced, but enthusiastic person who may take a positive view of corporate culture and attempt to incorporate this, to the older, more experienced, and battle-hardened individual whose interest lies in mentoring and developing the next group of leader, and all points in between!

▸ The experience of interacting with other teams has a pattern to it. There is a period of reflection about how the two teams may work together, what behavioral norms are and are not acceptable, and what roles each group will play. Much of the storming, forming, norming concept relates to this cultural challenge.

Taking a macro-perspective in looking for consistent cultural traits across an organization is often where transformation programs begin. However, ending the analysis there is likely to be a mistake.

What is the impact of national culture on transformation?

The literature on the above dimensions is considerable, from Trompenaar to Hofstede to Coyle. I don't propose to add to those, other than to provide two stories from two program directors, Paul Siegenthaler and John Monk. These stories illustrate, at a practical level, the impact of different national cultures on a critical part of any transformation program. In both these case studies, this was when the wider employee population was brought into the loop.

Paul Siegenthaler is a Swiss-born, German- and French-speaking scion of a classic mid-sized, family-owned business. As a result of acquisition, he entered the world of program leadership and has worked on a wide range of post-merger integration programs over the past twenty years, primarily in Europe. He has written an excellent book on the subject of merger integration: *Perfect M&A. The Art of Business Integration* (2009).

John was responsible for program-managing the divestiture of large parts of the global portfolio of Lloyds TSB, one of the UK's largest retail and commercial banks.

In this example, Paul is talking about the wholesale restructuring with a significant number of job losses at a boutique spirits manufacturer in Austria, and the response to the news.

'I was making an announcement about a wholesale restructuring in the Austrian business which was pretty dire; lots of people were going to lose their jobs. And at the end of it, everyone applauded. The HR person who had been sent

from London was stunned and wanted to make sure that they'd understood. So I asked the audience, why are you applauding? There was about five seconds of agonizing silence, and then one guy stood up and said, "This is a very coura-geous plan. Without it the whole company would go down. It's just a pity we didn't do this a few years ago." The HR person was amazed, and flew back to London and told everyone it had gone very well. As part of my response, I offered to speak to anyone on a one-to-one basis. The following day I had a queue outside my office; everyone wanted to speak. The key point that people in London did not understand is that if you'd had the same conversation with Spain or Italy, people would be at your throat, up in arms, but in that different Germanic culture, people do not express their emotions and they're certainly not going to discuss their personal issues in front of other people.'

In John Monk's example, he is describing the sale of a small Ecuadorian bank. The bank had been part of the Bank of London and South America business that was bought by Lloyds TSB and then sold as part of the restructuring following the merger with HBOS post financial crisis in 2010. The bank employed around two hundred and fifty people, and was an organization that many joined for life. The average tenure was twelve years, and the loyalty to the 'Black Horse' brand was extremely high. The business was well integrated in terms of systems, processes, and proce-dures. This is how he describes the response to the announcement of sale and his reaction and approach thereafter:

'For this deal to work, to retain value, we absolutely had to retain customers. Nothing else mattered and so keeping the planned sale quiet was critical. No one knew beyond the senior management. When the announcement was made, the scenes were really dramatic. There were people sobbing at the back when the announcement was made. I turned to my team and told them we needed to change the plan. It was clear that the one question that really mattered here that we had to deal with, the one question that the employees had in their heads, was, "How am I going to put food on the table for my family?"

The job became more than just a technical role. We had to be able manage people's emotions and their personal life as well as doing the job. We diverted a sizeable chunk of the budget to two activities, one focused on helping them with interview technique and the second helping them write their CVs. These guys, the local staff, had never had to do this before; it was a totally new experience for them.'

Is culture enough on its own?

Can a great culture by itself enable successful transformation? There are many examples in my interviews of organizations that demonstrate the power of specific corporate cultures in enabling transformation. There is one specific example, however, that is worth a brief description. This relates to a specific type of entrepreneur-led business, which has achieved a level of maturity in terms of size and market position but still maintains an incredibly flat structure and nimble decision-making process. It has an implementation skill set that is extraordinary. An example of this has emerged from a story about one of the leading food manufacturers in Southeast Asia. This organization had some unique characteristics.

▸ First, a 'learning agile' culture, based on an exceptionally close relationship between leadership and employee, which was based on trust and respect in both directions.
▸ Second, intuition in terms of decision making was perceived to be a key skill that needed to be encouraged and almost practiced.
▸ Third, autonomy and decentralization were at the heart of the culture with an expectation that those in decision-making positions responded quickly to the situations they were managing. All of this added up to a collective spirit that was remarkable and relatively non-hierarchical. A story from an interviewee gives some insight into that idea:

'I was attending a workshop at the offices when one of the kitchen staff started to bring in lunch for the delegates—a typically grand affair. As she tried to take various dishes from her oversized tray, the inevitable happened and food went literally everywhere. The first person to leap to her assistance was one of the most senior people in the company, who then proceeded to help clean up the mess.'

Like many of the examples above, this seems minor. One might easily attribute this to personality rather than corporate culture. It is not a silver bullet. To underestimate its relative importance would, however, be a mistake. Culture change begins and potentially ends at the micro level.

Leadership in good ecosystems

What type of leader do you need to run your transformation programs?
If culture has been the subject of endless academic and applied debate, the concept of and discussion around leadership is on an entirely different level! My contribution to this is based purely on observations around transformation.

There is a fundamental dichotomy at the heart of leadership selection for transformation programs.

▸ Individuals are selected for senior roles based on their perceived 'strategic' rational thinking capability.
▸ Without exception, the commentary around 'great' leaders is **not** focused on strategic decision making and clear headed rational thinking. It is instead largely about empathy, listening and communication skills, and loyalty. There are clearly some 'visionaries' out there. However, even these reflect the thoughts and ideas of those around them, recognizing sensibly enough that a vision without consensus to implement has no value.

To put the challenge succinctly, in transformation programs we admire and will follow leaders who have superior irrational 'human' skills. We recruit leaders, however, who outperform consistently with a skill set that is profoundly 'inhuman' in nature: the ability to disregard the challenge of implementation and identify an end state.

What leadership characteristics are present in transformation-friendly ecosystems?
Throughout the interviews, certain themes consistently present themselves. None of them are particularly earth-shattering. Most organizations would expect to have these characteristics. The difference, as ever, is in the reality, not the perception.

Open and honest...

Simon Clinton is a highly experienced Mergers and Acquisitions lawyer and ex head of Corporate at Clifford Chance for their Southeast Asia and Middle East regions as well as global head of the Sovereign Wealth sector. He has worked on some of the largest and most complex transactions around the world for more than twenty years. His insight as to what makes a successful acquirer is interesting, and a little surprising. He says:

> 'Those who are open and honest about their integration intentions are much more likely to be successful. From that comes the trust, inclusiveness, and engagement that are the fundamental building blocks behind integration.'

Charlie Johnstone, a partner from within the Private Equity world with a long track record of buying private businesses, provides another example of this. His language is typically 'financial engineering' as he tries to get his head around what success looks like in his investment history.

> 'We looked for a correlation of success factors. A particularly high correlation factor was that the businesses had a 'strong culture.' What we meant by that was that it had an open culture of honesty. Accountability is really the best way of describing it. And so we were constantly trying to think through how can you assess that? If they have an employee survey, that's a good sign because at least it means that they are starting to listen.
>
> The best businesses we backed had this wonderful high-performing culture, everyone pulling together. People could openly make mistakes. People were openly accountable for their own mistakes There was no pointing the finger at someone else. The person who was responsible needed to be honest about the mistake, but they were not going to be kicked for it.'

He goes on to describe the impact of that type of approach on performance:

> 'That enables them to take a risk in something not working. Their attitude is, that's what we do for a living. Those types of organizations are rare but very refreshing. If they're in a growing niche and they've got the right technology platform or proposition, they are much more likely to succeed, compared to their peers.'

This open and honest environment leads to a set of checks and balances where conflicts of interest are identified, acknowledged, and accounted for throughout a transaction. There is no attempt to nullify them. The focus is enabling a different mindset and point of view to be heard.

Simon's comment with regard to integration plans being shared with the business being acquired is a big step forward. For many organizations, allowing access during due diligence for internal integration teams to start forming views, developing plans, and identifying risks is a change in approach that many are reluctant to take. The concept that these plans might be shared with the seller is a big leap, but one which seems to be valuable in retaining value and goodwill.

Open…and receptive?

The biggest delta for many acquirers is the gap between what they think they know as a result of due diligence and the reality. Due diligence is a deeply flawed process. While the market may demand a detailed business case on announcement, the discovery process to underpin that business case usually only starts post completion. Being open in a post-deal integration program is being receptive to unknown opportunities.

Mark Stride led the Corporate Development team in Asia at Standard Chartered Bank (SCB) for five years before moving back to the UK to run the bank's global Investor Relations activities.

In his example, Mark describes a particularly successful acquisition of a small but fast-growing consumer credit business based in Hong Kong, a relatively lightly regulated segment of the market that SCB had not previously catered to. The intent was for the acquired company's founding management team to continue operating the business under its existing branding, but for the middle- and back-office operations to be aligned with that of SCB's much larger Hong Kong business. The hypothesis was that the smaller business's functions including risk management and compliance could benefit from the scale of the larger business, further improving its operational strength and financial performance.

In reality, it quickly became apparent to the integration team that the acquired business was consistently successful precisely because of its exceptional skill at assessing and managing risk on a much more agile and granular basis than SCB was used to with its relatively more affluent customer base. Rather than seek to impose its structure on the acquired entity, therefore, the integration team actually did the opposite, importing some of its best practices and technology to improve SCB's own functionality.

Being open and honest is hardly rocket science in terms of leadership! It is right up there with integrity and authenticity in the 'leadership for dummies' course structure. In the context of mergers and acquisitions, however, the insight is this:

> *The need for certainty comes precisely at the moment when there is the great-est degree of uncertainty. The good leader of transformation programs needs to create an atmosphere in which it's OK to say, 'I don't know.' And the best and only long-term way to do that is to demonstrate that behavior through his / her own actions.*

The role of the incomer / naysayer

Encouraging debate is a big part of being open, honest, and receptive. At its most extreme, that involves listening and acting upon the advice of someone who is challenging the status quo.

What drives this change in approach? It is remarkable how often a specific indi-vidual seems to be the main initiator for a change in momentum or approach. In many of these stories, there are a number of distinguishing features that relate to the personality or style of that individual:

- ▸ First, the individual has a history within the company of being a naysayer. He or she also has a track record of resolving difficult situations. There is an expec-tation that this is what they do.
- ▸ Second, despite their length of service, they maintain a difference in their method of working from the common culture of the organization. This differ-ence creates momentum and change. It also enables others with different perspectives to emerge.
- ▸ Thirdly they are superb communicators.

  Matthew Syed, in his recent book *Rebel Ideas,* writes about the power of the incomer, as someone who *'has the mental flexibility to bridge between*

> *domains; who sees the walls that we construct between disciplines and thought silos and regard them not as immutable but moveable, even breakable.'*

Is the role of the naysayer as much about the individual as it is about the organization? Can you recruit someone for that role, or is it more about the environment in which they are nurtured? The following two stories begin to answer those questions.

The first example is given by Melissa Almasi, whom we met earlier in the context of health and safety. In this case study, the transformation program scope was a separation and industry sale of non-core assets from a large primary industry market leader. These assets were operationally efficient and were generating a good return. They were, however, a draw on capital that could be used more effectively elsewhere.

Melissa speaks eloquently about the power and influence of the naysayer. The example below focuses on the inflection point that his introduction to the program heralded:

> 'The first thing that he challenged was the structure for the transaction. He asked me, "Are we doing it this way because the corporate strategy guys said that was the right structure...because they're idiots?" Then he started to question the whole nature of reporting, the red / amber / green measurement process. He introduced the concept of physical measures of progress. "I want to see the actual number of invoices the new shared service center has processed this week and the percentage they've achieved so that I can see the transition from RemainCo to NewCo."'

In the above example, the incomer's role is all about practical, pragmatic implementation. Challenging reporting processes is powerful, not just because it is the accepted norm in most major programs, but also because, as he implicitly recognizes, it changes the focus of what success looks like for the program as a whole. Measuring actual change becomes the benchmark.

In other situations, the incomer role is performed by the program director. Dean Cleland is the CEO for YOMA Bank, one of the leading private-sector banks based in Myanmar. Originally from New Zealand, Dean has worked across Southeast Asia and Australia in senior program director and business leadership roles throughout the banking sector.

He tells the story of being brought in to implement a major change program in the small and medium-sized sector for a bank in Australia.

'I was recruited to execute an SME strategy that had been developed by group strategy in consultation with the business. The problem they were trying to solve was how you keep human relationship intensity in a banking and finance context when the world is digitizing.

The senior executive who hired me positioned the program as "Dean, you literally need to pick up the strategy and execute it." "It" was a four-hundred-page PowerPoint pack. I read it and intuitively it didn't feel right to me. I had spent my life dealing with SME customers, and after reading the strategic paper I could see no rationale for the customer. We had over a million small business customers, and there was no way we could find enough relationship managers to give every small business customer someone to talk to. The strategy was to rethink the way we could keep the relationship intensity that had made us so successful but accommodate for the digital world.

What became clear was there was no real customer focus lens to it. When I asked the sponsor whether anyone had done any human-centered design or customer research, the answer was "No."'

When I ask him why he thinks they might have missed this, he has a simple answer:

'Most people who write strategy own the business, live in the business, and therefore fundamentally believe they know the business.'

In both the above cases, the people playing the 'incomer' role have quite similar characteristics. They are long-standing, senior employees with a track record of delivery. This gives them credibility and influence—a powerful combination.

Good ecosystems break down silos

For as long as I've been involved in M&A and transformation, there have been a number of accepted and mostly unchallenged rules. One of them is that we will run the program on a functional or silo basis. The logic is simple:

▸ It reflects the organization structure of most acquiring and acquired businesses, and it is well understood among stakeholders. It also reflects the existing governance structure.
▸ Functional expertise is established. It is logical, therefore, to pass the delivery responsibility to those subject-matter experts.
▸ Disruption to the organization is minimized by maintaining this particular norm.

This logic also plays to our own unwillingness to deal with uncertainty. Silos exist for a reason. There is a strange comfort that comes from working within a silo. We know the people of influence, we understand the critical skill set, we speak the language of the silo. The career path is easy to determine. Uncertainty becomes the exception rather than the rule.

As ever, what comes easiest is not always the right answer. In the context of post-deal implementation, there are some challenges to consider:

▸ Does the integration have deliverables that require certain functions to work together? For example, is there the intent to develop and deliver a new product roadmap in order to deliver against some cross-selling revenue synergies?
▸ In other deliverables, for example in achieving your new operating model, is there a need to bring together Technology, Property, and HR to deliver the envisaged benefits? Is there going to be a new location strategy that allocates work in the most cost-effective manner?
▸ How integrated are your various control functions? Risk, Compliance, Legal, and Finance have important actions to complete at the start of any integration program, particularly in regulated industries. In developing the right behavioral norms for your new employees, you might want to think about a limited set of consistent messages rather than four different presentations that look disjointed and confuse rather than clarify.

From my interviews, it would seem that organizations that are successful at transformation tend to be good at working across functions.

Working across functions

James Berry was the co-founder of Adastra, a software business that was started in 1994 to provide call management services for out-of-hours and clinical management within the UK health care sector. Ultimately the business became the software cornerstone of 911 / NHS Direct services in the UK and has remained a core part of the systems architecture for more than twenty years. Adastra was renamed Advanced Heath & Care and sold to Vista Equity Partners in 2015. James remained with the firm as transformation lead for Product Management and Engineering, as well as taking on a number of other non-executive and consulting engagements.

Gordon Craig was the co-founder of Craneware, a software business working as the integrated solution between US health care providers and the domestic health insurance market. The business was started in 1999 and listed on AIM in 2007. It currently serves more than one-third of all registered hospitals in the US.

Both James and Gordon focus on the critical nature of informal interactions between developers, product managers, and customer-facing people. Gordon gives a couple of examples of how that was ingrained in Craneware's culture:

> 'From the start, we kept communication open. Myself and Keith, for example, shared office space. For the first ten years of the company's history, you had the CTO and the CEO in the same room. I could overhear his conversations on the telephone and he could hear mine, we'd always pick up on various things.
>
> Until our move, we were always in open-plan. Everyone could see if a developer was fixing a bug and trying to get a release out of the door.
>
> Strangely, one of the best things I think I did as CTO was put a pool table into the office. What that does is bring testers, developers, and product managers. They don't chat about things going outside of work. The majority of the chat is about what they're doing, what they're not doing and maybe should be doing.'

Sandip Joshi is a program director within the investment banking sector and a subject matter expert in Risk management and Technology delivery. He brings experience in bringing together highly siloed environments where interests are often not shared and potentially diverge considerably. For him the face-to-face engagement process at the start of a complex delivery process was critical.

In this example, he is describing the roll-out of a global technology enabled change program, designed to create a single platform for consistency across different regions.

'We had people on the team from New York, London, Zurich, and India. The first thing we did was have a workshop in India where we got the whole team together to work on the next level of planning. We literally spent the whole week just on planning. The payback on that time? It was extraordinary. Bringing the team together face-to-face, looking each other in the eye, making sure everyone had the same understanding of priorities. Not just implementers, everyone from the product owner to the global head of the function. It didn't matter what stream you worked in, we were all in the room together. We went through the technical development, the data aspects, the whole user and migration training aspect. Everyone was involved in the planning process, regardless of whether they were directly involved in that stream or not. And what that gave people was a lot of context. They could see how their individual pieces contributed to the overall success.'

The examples above are about building trust through a process of working together and establishing a common goal. The functional bond is replaced by the program bond.

Small visible signs of change...the 'optics'

Organizations that do change well often start small. The impact of a small change in behavior can be significant. This is particularly the case with leadership behavior: changing the format of a meeting so that the most junior person there gets to be heard first; changing personal working hours to reflect the corporate stated ambition of work / life balance; reducing personal air travel to respond to carbon footprint reduction goals. By themselves these are not earth-shattering, but their impact is magnified because leaders have themselves undertaken the change.

As ever, the challenge is consistency.

In my interview with a senior program director with experience in transformation and COO roles in the UK industrial and manufacturing world, he described two situations that illustrate the challenge of consistency perfectly:

> 'We've got margins of 3%, but we're flying twenty people first-class to Australia next month. We have tea ladies who bring tea round to everybody twice a day in their offices. If I want to convince a manager that he needs to fire someone who's only earning forty grand a year, then I need to show him the strategic intent to reduce the costs in this business. And that means the tea ladies, it means that I'm not going to fly first class. It means that the secretaries aren't going to have company cars. It means that I'm not going to employ twenty security guys. There are lots of things that you can do to show the strategic intent that the business needs to change the way in which it has behaved for the last forty years.

> I went into a business with a very experienced management team that had been there for a very long time. The MD sat in his wood-paneled office in a building divorced from manufacturing with a secretary in another wood-paneled office right next to him. She brings in his tea in the morning at 10.30 and his lunch in on a tray at 12.30. It's not just him, everybody was treated like that. He has his parking spot right outside the front door, etc. And this is a business that was losing money...they're paying a secretary £23,000 a year to do about ten hours of work a week delivering food and hot drinks to the senior leadership. The organization had not changed in thirty years. How can you possibly expect others to change when they see that kind of waste?'

I asked him about the state of the business when he left:

> 'By the end of the three years I was there, the only two functions left in the office block were Finance and Customer Services. Everybody else was in the middle of the factory. I'm sitting in the shop floor, we are making this change, and if you're doing something that doesn't fit with the change, I'm going to challenge you.

> *I had one production engineer who was incredible. We used to make two types of valve used in a central heating system. Over the three-year period, one production engineer with his team of people on the line increased the output on a units per person per day basis by 92% with zero capital investment. There were twenty-two people on the line originally, they reduced it down to seven while increasing throughput at the same time.'*

That's not the only time the theme of the 'optics' arises. One of my interviewees talks about the office space very openly:

> *'I remember going to the client in the beginning of the process, to this crappy office outside London and thinking, "no wonder no one wants to transform. This place sucks the life out of you." And you look at this other organization located in this dump of an office in Victoria, and now they've moved their location into Tottenham Court Road, fantastic offices. It doesn't feel like a slow, sluggish public sector services business. It feels like a dynamic, technology-enabled place. The optics are often overlooked.'*

These are just a few examples of the power of 'optics.' The more time I spend with the interviewees, the more examples they were able to remember of these types of small change. There is often a sense of embarrassment that these actions really contributed to the overall change.

It does not sit easily with many of us in the world of program management that the key to change is not large or eye-catching. The evidence from my interviews suggests it is be the reality.

Decentralization and autonomy

Organizations that deliver transformation successfully are comfortable with vesting decision making to the appropriate level. This is the place where the expertise and the requirement actually coincide. The challenge is whether the divestment of control is real or imagined.

Control is a deceptive thing. If you are in a leadership team, it is easy to persuade yourself that ownership requires control. Being in control justifies your position. Going from being the visionary to the person controlling implementation is a very small step in a process flow, but a very large step in the organizational psyche. Scale has absolutely no bearing on this except in one important dimension. Centralized control becomes harder and harder the bigger you get. It also generates a bunch of unattractive side effects which you probably do not want.

Paul Siegenthaler describes the challenge well. In the case of Diageo, the size, scale, and ambition of leadership in terms of integration created an environment where decentralized decision making was perceived as critical:

> 'What I discovered early on was that when you've got integration happening in lots of different and unrelated markets, you've got to document the decision-making criteria rather than making the decisions yourself. That really speeds things up, it stops the question, "How did you get to that conclusion?" All operational decisions like location or which system to use are based on those criteria and it becomes a real accelerator.'

My conversation with a head of portfolio within a large multinational organization brought one of those moments where clarity of thought, self-realization, and humility seemed to come together. Here is how he describes his organization in terms of the new approach:

> 'My organization is going through a massive transformation in terms of how we do business, We've realized that what we have done previously may not be sustainable in the future. And so we are slowly transforming our organization to becoming more agile. We have essentially restructured ourselves into becoming networks, both internally and in the way that we develop value for our patients outside of the organization. It's happening in the downstream where we make and sell our products, but it's also happening upstream in the discovery phase.'

It's easy to be cynical about this objective. There are many organizations globally that have promised this type of transformation and delivered very little. Here's how he describes the implementation phase, in particular the point about perceived control:

'The idea of the transformation, the way that we have come together, and the model that we have created had very little leadership involvement. It was up to the middle and the bottom layer to model it all. We were given guard rails "where you can operate, you decide what you want to do." Of course, there were lots of challenging questions along the way from leadership. Those are helpful, they keep us in balance, but it's our journey.

There are a few pretty bold actions early on. First, decisions are now being pushed down to the lowest level of the organization. To give an example, our local (country-based) operations are now completely empowered to make decisions because they are the closest to the market. You don't have to go to the regional office to make decisions. So as long as you are fully aware and you are transparent about it, you are empowered and encouraged to make the decision. The second thing is that we have adopted an iterative approach in terms of how we want to scale things. There is an understanding that we will need to change as we implement.

Third, the middle layer has been removed. In the regional office where I am based we've reduced numbers significantly. We have also condensed the geographies that used to create a lot of territorial mindset into just two geographies, US and Rest of the World.'

I asked him to talk through the challenges of that transformation, for him personally and for the organization as a whole.

'While the spirit of what we're trying to achieve is noble and great, I do find it difficult from a human perspective. I've been accustomed to working in a particular way throughout my life in the traditional organization where I'm clear on what I need to do from a job description perspective. I'm clear in terms of what KPIs need to be achieved. For example, in the past we focused our attention doing value maintenance work as opposed to value creation.

But now everything is turned up the other way around. I have to define it myself. I need to identify what the value creation opportunity is, even if I don't know that at the start. I need to ensure that I set myself up in a particular *set of behaviors where I can engage with others and co-create that level of value creation.*

I personally struggle when my manager who sits in Canada says, "You're fully empowered." That's exciting and that's motivating. But empowerment also can take a different meaning altogether. I have realized that empowerment has also allowed me to be a little complacent at times, that I've missed on a few key deliverables because of this skewed interpretation of empowerment in my head. I have needed a good colleague of mine to come and nudge me a few times and say, "Hey, you know what? You really have not done this. You've got to step up on this."'

What about his role as a head of portfolio? How has the change impacted on those who look to him for guidance and direction?

'I've just come off a call with a colleague from Indonesia who was asking me, "How would I do this? How should I do this? Can you direct me, point me to the step by step way of doing this?" and I'm holding myself back saying that this is potentially how you should think about it. Although at the back of my mind I know exactly what she should be doing, I want her to think for herself and make that jump so that she can then take ownership of the value of what she's trying to deliver.

Now I am more focused on ensuring that I challenge each and every initiative from a business value standpoint, which I didn't previously do. What I do less is embed myself in a place where I'm challenging the process, "Have you followed this step, that process? Show me your resource map. Show me your risk management. Where's your risk log?"'

The power in this story is that it describes a very personal journey and the impact of radical decentralization on a successful middle manager and long-term employee.

Communications – engaging with the organization

The reason for communications coming at the end of this chapter is not that communication is not important. It is because the approach to it is a culmination of all the other themes explored in this chapter.

In my golf story in the Introduction to this book, I wrote about the difference between strategy and implementation. In the context of communications, one might describe that as the difference between perception of successful information flow and the reality of what is actually being understood.

Good communications in transformation are less about doing things exceptionally well and more about not making the same mistakes again and again. The common communications theme for organizations that are good at transformation is a lack of complacency. They recognize that just because we as humans spend our lives communicating, this doesn't necessarily mean that we are always good at it.

I have set out below some of the challenges that organizations face in transformation.

What is the right channel and why does it matter?
Choosing the right channel of communication is more challenging than ever in these days of mass media and a myriad different delivery methods, all of which are competing for the same short window of attention.

The basic premise regarding channel or method is simple but perhaps startling:

What you say is entirely immaterial if no one hears you

Some examples:

▸ Sending an email to the entire workforce in a single location about an impending fire practice is appropriate. Sending an email to the entire workforce asking them to change their behavior as part of a cultural change program is pointless. It might suit the messenger but have minimal impact on the recipient.
▸ Using a newsletter to give the acquired employees an update on integration is

an enormous effort for very little benefit. First, the majority of the information will be out of date given the inevitable editorial process involved in producing the artefact. Second, the more 'formal' the channel looks, the more it relies on trust. In an integration, trust of the acquiring leadership takes a long time to establish.

▸ Arranging a town hall meeting that is almost entirely Q&A based with little 'obvious' preparation for senior leadership is incredibly powerful in the building of relationships. More importantly, it starts the flow of feedback as employees become more confident in their ability to ask challenging questions and get honest answers.

Listening starts at the top

There is a universal acceptance these days that the role of leadership in transformation is primarily one of issue resolution and communication. In the Nextel example, the effort required to do the latter effectively is made really clear. While the time taken by Roberto Rittes to connect with employees is impressive, the time taken to prepare and respond post event is not included. In his case, communications were the single largest use of his time by far.

There is an inherent challenge in thinking about communications at leadership level. Think about your immediate reaction when you looked at the subject title. If, like me, your immediate thought was about delivery of messages rather than listening, you're probably in the majority. Our expectation is that leadership talks and the rest listen.

In companies that do transformation well, however, there is a clear trend that suggests that listening is a behavior that is established most successfully from the top. It's not easy, though.

Everyone talks about being a good listener. Few talk about the complexity and specific behavioral challenges that underpin that capability. Even fewer talk about the effort involved, which is considerable. In many companies, organizational structure becomes a blockage rather than an enabler for listening. Echo chambers abound at senior level in organizations. Messengers continue to be shot! Hierarchy obfuscates rather than clarifies what really needs to be heard.

Paul Siegenthaler captures the challenge well when he talks about real consultation.

> 'If people understand what's being decided, why it's been decided, what were the alternatives, and even if one of the alternatives would have been much more pleasant for them, if they understand how that fits into the general picture, they are in most cases mature enough to agree to disagree.'

So the key thing is how do they react to those below them?

> 'Yes. The reaction you want to avoid to their colleagues or those who report into them is "It's the top floor. They don't know what real life is. If they had asked me, I would've told them X, Y, Z." That just destroys trust, and then you're in trouble'.

Friction – the barrier to great communications

In organizations, friction is the static. It is the seemingly meaningless obstruction that prevents change from taking place. It is the duplication of data input in several different systems, it is the maintenance of a process whose purpose has been lost long ago but that still has a key performance indicator attached, it is the publication of a newsletter that no one reads but which requires enormous personal intervention and editorial time to 'set the right tone.' It is the floor plan that puts two functions at opposite ends of a building because no one has thought to challenge it. Friction is the ultimate, subtle, invisible destroyer of innovation and employee engagement.

Sometimes friction has a really meaningful impact.

Post the financial crisis in 2008, there was much discussion as to why certain investment banks had performed badly and others hadn't.

The explanation of 'distance from the situation on the ground' in the case of mortgage defaults was often cited for cases like Morgan Stanley or indeed Lehman Brothers. The concept is a simple one:

- ▸ The information flow for trading decisions came through a series of intermediaries such as estate agents, local banks reporting on default rates, local newspapers starting to comment, and finally analysts putting the story together.
- ▸ If that was how traders were receiving information, then in terms of speed of response, the information was coming out very late.
- ▸ In organizations that were removed from the 'situation on the ground,' that is,

they did not have the relationships or analytical focus on the above intermediaries, traders would be effectively responding to information that was already out of date.

What about the situation with banks that had a business unit that was specifically focused on mortgage lending? Surely, for organizations like that, they would be able to get this information much faster as the sources were internal.

It turns out that that was not the case. Citibank, one of the largest players in the mortgage securities marketplace, and a very significant provider of mortgages to small-town America, suffered as badly as those who were at an information flow disadvantage. Why? The reason is simple.

Despite their employer being the same, it turns out that the average New York based mortgage securities trader does not have a lot in common with someone in Florida who has an informed view of mortgage default rates in their patch. You can just imagine the conversation between them as the organizational hierarchy plays out.

You might say that this is as much about size as it is about hierarchy. How can an organization of more than two hundred and fifty thousand people possibly hope to maintain that kind of connectivity? I would suggest that if the mortgage administrator in Florida had a burning desire to inform the trader in New York about the marketplace, finding an access point through their network wouldn't be a challenge. The three key words here however are 'desire,' 'access,' and 'credibility.'

- ▸ 'Desire' because the administrator in Florida needs to feel engaged with their employer to want to share their insight with someone whom they don't know and where they have no influence.
- ▸ 'Access' so that in the event they do want to pick up the phone to the trader in New York, they may actually have a chance of getting through.
- ▸ 'Credibility' so that, in the event that they get through, the trader actually takes what they say seriously.

It is worth thinking about the friction in your own organization and the impact it may be having on the flow of information both upward and downward. Removing friction is an important aspect of any attempt to improve transformation. Its impact on communications specifically should not be underestimated.

. . . .

Communications in transformation is a subject that needs more focus than I'm able to provide here. The key theme is clear, however. Successful communication is a collective effort, not an individual one. It is dependent on a constant flow of information that is both qualitative and quantitative. Strategy and implementation evolve as a consequence of trial and error. Without direct and fast communications across, upward, and downward, that evolution is going to stall.

Conclusion

Does what is good in the context of transformation differ widely from what is good in the 'business-as-usual' world? In part. The pressures of transformation and change highlight weaknesses in an organization that are not so obvious in the steady state. Organizations that are transforming need to set themselves very high standards in the context of communications capability and organizational flexibility. These high standards are likely to have a positive impact on business as usual as well.

There is another consideration. Many organizations achieve success in the first or second transformation attempts. The level of stakeholder engagement, focus, and corporate will to succeed can be enough to achieve the key objectives. If you believe that transformation and change are temporary, that is probably enough. If, on the other hand, you think that transformation is the new normal, the challenge is a different one.

It lies in the collective willingness to maintain the corporate learning capability, appetite, and flexibility that sits at the heart of successful transformation. It is this backbone that the ecosystem provides—a backbone that has the potential to outlast any existing incumbent leader and truly become part of the DNA of the business.

05
THE 'DARK' SIDE OF THE ECOSYSTEM: TOXIC ENVIRONMENTS AND THEIR IMPACT ON TRANSFORMATION

Like many in my profession, I have long been a proponent of the concept that corporate and team cultures cannot, of themselves, be good or bad: that a binary definition like that is neither helpful nor correct; that we should describe a way of working or a corporate culture in non-pejorative language; that we should accept that things just get done differently in different places.

This is a safe place to operate in. You minimize the possibility of offense, which as a consultant is pretty important. You massage leadership egos. You move on to quietly change and discard the elements of the culture that are causing a problem.

Enough! In the spirit of openness and accountability that is reflected in the vast majority of the stories from a set of interviewees who were kind enough to let me into their lives and experiences and share what they'd done well or badly, I need to do the same.

We need to get away from that safe place and tell it how it is. There are some corporate ecosystems that are toxic to major transformation programs and post-deal integrations. The consequence of pursuing these types of activities in those ecosystems is going to be failure. That failure is not something to disregard. While it may have a detrimental impact on shareholder returns, its real and long-term impact is on the morale, productivity, and potential mental health of employees.

These are not things that can be turned around next quarter or next year. They have a long-term impact.

In this chapter I'm going to let the stories from my interviewees speak about what constitutes a toxic ecosystem. I am also going to let them explain how, in many cases, these were changed, and how the changes had an impact on performance, employee productivity, and transformation success.

A note of caution. It is easy to read these stories as anecdotes and trivialize them as not being reflective of the organizations as a whole. To repeat my comment, qualitative data has an important place in any review process. It is a part of the picture for management professionals and leaders. I trust the experience, knowledge, and integrity of those who have given me their insights. I would urge you to do the same.

You will not be surprised that for the purposes of this chapter, most of my interviewees wanted to stay anonymous. The stories will remain so as well.

What, then, are the characteristics of transformation-toxic ecosystems? What insights can we gain from those who have tried and often failed to implement transformation programs in these organizations?

Autocracy and a lack of fairness

A key theme relates to the decision-making process and a lack of care for the employee base. Humans are hardwired to judge the fairness of an action or decision. Its perceived absence tends to overpower anything positive.

One of my interviewees is a principal from a medium-size private equity firm with more than fifteen years' experience. He is an operations partner with a specific focus on turnaround and operational improvement. For him, much of the starting point for operational efficiency sits within the finance / HR and technology functions. He tells the story of a business that he backed as a private equity investor. From an investment perspective, the opportunity was an excellent one, but he and his partners were aware of the cultural challenges from the start.

'The interesting thing was that most of the market and quite a few of the entrepreneurs in the sector responded quite openly with a sense of shock. "Oh my

God, someone's finally bought this." "They are going to be shafted by this."
They had a pretty shocking reputation.'

He then goes on to give some insight into the culture of the business.

'They had a very autocratic culture. A really good example of that was the call
center. It was located in the head office building on the top floor, a couple
of floors above the leadership team. None of the leadership team had ever
gone up there. The turnover of staff in the call center was more than 100%
per annum, which you'd think would be a good reason to have a look around
and speak to some people!

A few things became obvious really early on. Nearly everyone in the call center
would bring in their own food to put in the microwave. But there was only one
microwave for something like eighty people! When each section had their
lunch, people might have to queue for half an hour before they could even put
their food in for what was only a forty-five-minute lunch break. No one had
thought to buy them another.

At the Christmas party, the founders sat at the top table with different food
and high-quality wine, and invited their trusted people around them. The next
section down was the white-collar workers, who were given less good wine
and food. The top table got to take the next day off, the white-collar workers
had half a day. And then you had the call center workers who had the cheapest
of everything and would have to go into work the next day. It was extraordinary,
and really set the tone for the organization.'

So what happened when you arrived? What was the reaction to private equity?

'It's an interesting question. The thing about the culture there was that it wasn't
just benign neglect. There was some real nastiness in there. When they sold
it to us, one of the last things they said to the staff as they were leaving was,
"You thought we were bad; just you wait until you get these private equity
bastards in."'

It is easy to think about this story as an isolated incidence. The actions taken by the new leadership team are not hard to imagine...buying a couple of new microwaves, the CEO regularly walking the floor, restructuring the call center staff based on some analysis of individual and team performance....none of this is particularly earth-shattering. The improvement in performance was extraordinary, and staff turnover went from over 100% to around 30%, which is remarkable.

The point to note is that the culture in this organization did not just arise overnight. It is the result of a long and sustained period of neglect where one action led to another, with the result as detailed above. The opportunity for a 'naysayer,' in this case private equity, is to look at the specific with a different lens and identify immediate opportunities for change.

The customer...and a faster horse

On the dark side of the ecosystem, customers are often seen as necessary but ultimately inconvenient. In a recent conversation with a COO responsible for the largest integration in the company's history, when asked about the customers, his response was flat: *'That's not a priority on this transaction. We'll deal with them later.'*

What drives this response?

▸ The first is the perception that customers will want either no change at all or something that is not deliverable. It is better therefore that we don't ask them. The analogy of 'Pandora's box' is frequently mentioned in this context.
▸ The second view is that customers are basically stupid. This is rarely stated directly these days, following the Ratner debacle. It does, however, remain part of corporate narrative. Below is some paraphrased commentary from my interviews that captures this particular dimension:

  - 'What we do is so complicated and challenging that it is unlikely that anyone outside of this organization could possibly understand it.' (Data management company.)
  - 'We hold the keys to innovation here because we lead the industry with our talent and technology. Where we go, customers will follow.' (Financial services infrastructure company.)
  - 'The friction to move to another provider of similar services is very high (and

we have no reason to reduce it). Our customer base is extremely sticky as a consequence. By consulting with them, we potentially open their eyes to the possibility of going elsewhere.' (Utility.)

- 'All the innovation being offered by our competitors is already available to them in our product and service. It's a question of them just asking us and we can do it for them.' (Private banking.)

▸ The third dimension is simply around the length of relationship. The logic is that changing a relationship gets more difficult the longer the relationship has been in place, which in turn leads to poor customer care and uncompetitive pricing.

One of my conversations was with a head of Corporate Strategy in the financial services sector, based in Scandinavia. His experience includes time with the Big Four as a strategic advisor, before a long spell in-house with one of the largest Nordic banking groups. Subsequently he has also worked with private equity as a strategy partner.

His story relates to the positioning of the customer. In this case, it was a large domestic bank contemplating a major systems change as the first step in a major post-merger integration program. The question raised around the board table related to customer experience and the potential value of creating some kind of feedback loop. One particularly influential board member dismissed the idea. His comment was, *"If you had asked a customer two hundred years ago what he wanted, he would have said a faster horse."*

For many organizations struggling with transformation programs, external feedback is rare because it is largely unwanted. Feedback is seen as a distraction from the intent of the program, has limited value, and takes valuable resources from core activities with stressed timelines.

A foundation made of sand…poor business sponsorship and a fragile business case

The connection between management sponsorship and business case has always been powerful. Without a clear benefit, it is hard to find someone who is prepared to commit to the work and the spend. The issue in organizations that are poor at transformation stems from a lack of accountability. If you have a solid business case, finding a management sponsor is easy. Keeping them as the inevitable challenges of implementation unfold is considerably harder. The choice of sponsorship becomes a political one, rather than one based on ownership and commitment.

Konstantin Strangas is a senior program manager with more than ten years' experience in Asia. He has spent more than fifteen years in the world of outsourcing, working both as a consultant with the Big Four and in various in-house roles for large global corporates.

The context of the example below is the development of an outsourced center in Malaysia. The movement to Asia of outsourced support services has been established for more than thirty years, initially based on the delta in employment costs between developed and developing markets.

Kon comments on the fragility of a business case: a fragility that was based on behavior and the willingness to cooperate rather than any financial logic.

> 'We first went to Finance to talk about Accounts Payable as an entirely logical and commercially viable function to put into our new center. There was a precedent in our US model and a rock-solid business case. When I come back six months later, the slightest excuse is used to back out. Leadership says, 'We don't have enough reassurance and therefore we will continue to run it on a local to local basis.' I'm going from function to function, trying to make the case for centralization. And then the momentum changes because senior stakeholders are starting to doubt the process. They are asking you to bring the return timeline in, when literally three months earlier, everyone was in complete agreement.'

How did you turn it around?

> 'The thing that saved the project was someone we'd just hired who was enlightened enough to understand what I was getting at. She was responsible for talent management. She agreed that they would centralize for candidate screening and sourcing. I got scope but it fell into my lap. The business case does not show you the informal negotiation, all the time you need to take to make certain ideas palatable to individuals.'

Elina Niemela, whom we met in the section on process, has some interesting insights on the impact of delay on business performance. She talked to me about a recent program involving the 'non-integration' of a number of businesses bought five and ten years ago. In this case, the absence of a decision to integrate had a number of consequences.

▶ First, very different expectations and standards of delivery from the different entities that made cross-selling extremely difficult and any commercial negotiations around the overall offering to customers virtually impossible.
▶ Second, no commitment to the parent company at local leadership or employee level such that all the benefits of being part of a larger business had mostly been forgotten.

Ultimately, the issue in both of the examples above has nothing to with business case. It is about ownership and accountability, two behaviors which are fundamental in any organization wishing to succeed in transformation.

Poor decision making and the echo chamber

It turns out that organizations that struggle in transformation programs do so not because of poor decision making, but because of no decision making! In some cases the layers of management and governance create a situation where timeliness is virtually impossible. Is that by accident or by design? Part of this is down to the echo chamber that leadership inhabits.

The concept of the echo chamber has been explored at length in the world of social media. It has also been explored as the reason for failure in corporate life as internal challenge and discourse is replaced by homogeneity and reinforcement.

In organizations that struggle with transformation, the echo chamber is firmly established around the dominant personality. Challenge is discouraged and there are many myths and legends related to those who tried. Control in certain key areas (notably recruitment) is absolute.

Resourcing...everyone is an expert at recruiting

I can think of a number of occasions where I have been recruited for a role or consulting brief which I would not have given myself! On each occasion, the process was typical in that it came through my network of contacts. These same contacts provided a reference for the person hiring me, and the only real point of enquiry, in terms of an interview, was terminated early. Language like the following was used: *'I don't have any questions for you. If X and Y have recommended you, that's good enough for me.'*

This is not an unusual experience, and it reflects a basic failing in senior level program resourcing.

Recruiting one-off transformation roles is difficult in any case. Relying on the traditional recruitment process with interviews as the primary decision point makes it even harder. The process presupposes that the business knows what it is looking for. It also anticipates that the interviewer has the ability to differentiate between those who can deliver against the brief and those who cannot.

Recruiting the right people to support a program of transformation is challenging at the best of times. It becomes virtually impossible if the leaders of the organization have limited experience of implementing successful transformation previously.

Being removed from the marketplace...or being isolated

It is interesting that the concept of leadership being a lonely experience is often cited as one of the crosses that a leader *has* to bear. The concept of the pyramid where the top echelons are occupied by very few people works well in traditional organizational design discussions. Sadly, it also reflects traditional office design where the real estate assigned to people at the top of the organization reinforces that isolation.

The key point about leadership in transformation, however, is that this isolation is a choice, not a requirement. In many of the stories around failure, this self-imposed isolation leads to a total lack of understanding or an unwillingness to recognize fundamental flaws in the execution capability of an organization.

Relying on externals

Another consequence of this isolation is the increasing dependence on 'external' advisors. The success of strategic consulting is based on building very strong relationships at the top of the organization. These relationships are clearly valuable. For the leader, an external perspective is important and provides context for direction and market positioning. For the consultancy, the commercial value of that kind of relationship cannot be underestimated.

It is no surprise, then, that the delivery of transformation programs in organizations with bad ecosystems are often run and sometimes led by external consultants. Consultants come with a number of advantages:

▶ They are not permanent. For organizations with an autocratic decision-making culture, temporarily giving up that control to an external force can be attractive, in particular where the consulting business has a strong brand. The brand provides a convenient excuse for failure!

▶ Consultant and leadership team have vested interests. Both clearly want to be successful in program delivery but for the consultant, providing a challenge to a flawed process is a risky business. In an autocratic culture, the same rules apply for externals as internals: broadly, 'my way or the highway.' For a consultant, risking a potentially lucrative income stream by challenging a dominant leader is not a strategy that makes much sense.

There are some fundamental challenges for leadership in organizations that are poor at transformation:

▶ First, getting a leadership team to admit a lack of experience requires a special type of culture. With any uncertainty, bluster and bravado dominate. The environment becomes one where any kind of challenge as to the approach being taken is seen as a challenge to leadership. The echo chamber that tends to dominate in these types of organizations reinforces the dominant person's thinking and approach.

▶ Decisions regarding resourcing are based on intuition rather than knowledge and experience. Priorities are not challenged, resource plans are rarely checked, timelines remain theoretical.

▶ Recruitment for relevant and experienced resources, which is already difficult, is challenged further with some major constraints. A shortlisted candidate cannot:

  - challenge the 'established' principles of the program;
  - appear to provide an alternative and credible experience.

> ▸ Informal networks, particularly those of the dominant personality, tend to be the primary source of talent. As a consequence, there is no incentive for any internal check and balance given the implied challenge to the leader. While there are requirements these days to advertise internally and externally to show diligence in any recruitment process, it is still relatively easy to 'work' the system.

Conclusion

Confronting failure is not easy. Acknowledging systemic issues is unlikely to be career-enhancing for the individual. Post-mortems are often ineffective because there is no appetite for real corporate soul-searching. It is much easier to think about the future and imagine a better place.

Sadly, that is the perfect recipe for repeating the same mistakes. If there is one thing that is repeatedly mentioned in the interviews, and sits at the heart of any transformation failure, it is false optimism. Leadership continues to overestimate capability, capacity, and appetite for change. Right to left planning still dominates in transformation programs, where outcomes and timing are determined by leadership, in many cases disregarding the input of those with implementation responsibility.

The fear of failure needs to be confronted and acknowledged. A final anecdote that perhaps illustrates the challenge most vividly:

One of my interviewees described the process of giving a project update to key sponsors a couple of months into a two-year transformation program. Project updates are a regular part of the cadence of reporting issues, risks, and any specific challenges that need escalation.

On this occasion however, the preparation of a sixteen-page update to a regular steering committee took a hundred and twenty-four iterations, in effect a hundred and twenty-four nuanced versions of the same information. The chance of program success, even at this early stage, was minimal.

06
CONCLUSION

This book is about change. Change only happens at a personal level. Organizations change because individuals within them make a proactive decision to do something in a different way.

Our relationship with change is complicated. On the one hand, there is extraordinary awareness of its impact. Everyone knows about the change curve. The concept that 'change is the only constant' is often quoted as the basis on which we need to live our lives. On the other hand, change is uncomfortable. It is disruptive and destabilizing. Resistance to change is often expressed as some kind of heroic action. The word 'resistance,' particularly in the context of conflict, is seen as an act of courage and bravery, against all odds. Major political movements of the last ten years play to the desire to return to some kind of glorious past, whether that is the Empire and the discussions of sovereignty in the context of Brexit, or the glorious industrial past of the US under the leadership of Trump. We are drawn to the new, but hanker for the comfort of the old.

The three strategies identified in this book reflect this complex relationship.

Purpose is, by its very nature, holistic. It permeates the organization completely, so much so that anything that looks out of place is easily identifiable. It speaks to an employee directly in terms of ownership and engagement. It says, 'if you believe in me, then you are welcome to commit to me. Your commitment is demonstrated through your continued challenge...as an equal owner, it is your responsibility to be my custodian and to fight fiercely for my preservation and my purity.'

Process is more prosaic. It is task-based. It likes linearity. It likes the idea that an action leads to a result. It is an approach that is not prepared to address the big challenges of the organization unless those are complete adherence to a set of rules and procedures. It looks at a change and asks the question, 'How can I achieve this without disrupting everything else? How can I insulate the organization from this change so that only those directly affected feel the impact?' Its intent is honorable but conservative. There is always a sense in a process-led transformation that the business will return to something stable at the end, and everyone can breathe a sigh of relief.

Plasticity is a state of mind. It looks for sterility, ossification, and embedded processes and asks the question, 'Why? Why do we need that stability, why has that function never changed when all around it everything else has? Why do we need that process?' Plasticity challenges the idea of status quo with every fiber of its being.

Process, purpose, and plasticity are the foundations for transforming organizations. Purposeful organizations continue for as long as their purpose remains relevant. Companies with plasticity exist to challenge the established way of doing things. They exist for as long as constant change is desirable and energizing. Process-oriented companies achieve change in small increments. They exist in sectors that are stable: sectors where demand is constant and operational efficiency is the primary way of improving performance.

This book is also about the human experience of being responsible for a transformation program: taking the vision and strategy of an individual or a small team and turning it into reality. That journey is complicated.

Transformation is a messy, iterative, mistake-ridden process. It is a process where structure follows rather than leads, where strategy is constantly reinterpreted and often changed to fit success in implementation. It is a process where traditional power structures, organizational charts, and hierarchy become meaningless and where engagement becomes the critical element. For those involved, finding something to hold on to when everything else is moving is a challenge.

So why do it? Why engage? Why embrace the disruption? For those interviewed in the writing of this book, the answer is simple. For them, working on a transformation program provides them with intellectual and emotional stimulus. It gives them a daily dose of progress toward a common goal. And ultimately, it gives them a community that they can help to form and influence. A community that values them personally and professionally. A community that makes their professional lives fulfilling. In a world where transformation is rapidly becoming a core corporate skill set, encouraging the development of that community may be the first and most valuable step in the ongoing journey of change.

INDEX

Printed in Great Britain
by Amazon

64552442R00099